Sew Red

SEWING & QUILTING FOR WOMEN'S HEART HEALTH

LAURA ZANDER

FOREWORD BY DEBORAH NORVILLE

 sixth&springbooks NEW YORK

 **DEDICATION**

To Wiley and Buddy, our best friends who were taken from this earth too soon. Our hearts ache every single day for you.

 sixth&springbooks

161 Avenue of the Americas, New York, NY 10013
sixthandspringbooks.com

Editorial Director
JOY AQUILINO

Art Director
DIANE LAMPHRON

Editor
MARTHA MORAN

Developmental Editor
LISA SILVERMAN

Copy Editor
MICHÈLE FILON

Design & Art Production
LOIRA WALSH

Designer
JOY MAKON

Illustrations
ULI MONCH

Model Photography
ROSE CALLAHAN

Still-Life Photography
MARCUS TULLIS

Fashion Stylist
& Bookings Director
KHALIAH JONES

Hair & Makeup
SOKPHALLA BAN

....

Vice President, Publisher
TRISHA MALCOLM

Creative Director
JOE VIOR

Production Manager
DAVID JOINNIDES

President
ART JOINNIDES

Library of Congress Cataloging-in-Publication Data

Zander, Laura.
Sew red : sewing for women's heart health / by Laura Zander. — First edition
        p. cm.
ISBN 978-1-936096-55-8
1. Sewing. 2. Exercise therapy. I. Title.
TT705.Z36 2012
646'.34—dc23
        2012038944

MANUFACTURED IN CHINA

1 3 5 7 9 10 8 6 4 2

First Edition

The Heart Truth®, its logo and The Red Dress are registered trademarks of HHS.

Participation by Jimmy Beans Wool does not imply endorsement by HHS/NIH/NHLBI.

Contents

HOP! SKIP! JUMP!
page 12
❤ *Denyse Schmidt*

SPIRAL SCARF
page 16
❤ *Nancy Zieman*

SNOWBALL TABLE
RUNNER
page 20
❤ *Aneela Hoey*

YOU ARE SO LOVED
page 23
♥ *Vanessa Christenson*

CHATEAU NECKLACE
page 26
♥ *Kaari Meng*

ASIAN MODERN PILLOW
page 29
♥ *Linda Lee*

PATHFINDER QUILT
page 32
♥ *Valori Wells*

VILLAGE BAG
page 37
♥ *Me and My Sister Designs*

PANELED MAXI SKIRT
page 42
♥ *Ellen March*

FLEUR ROUGE QUILT
page 46
♥ *Anna Griffin*

PARSON GRAY DITTY BAG
page 51
♥ *David Butler*

HEARTFELT ROSY
page 54
♥ *Kaffe Fassett*

ORIGAMI PILLOW
page 58
♥ *Brett Bara*

KIMONO SLEEVE TUNIC
page 61
♥ *Suede*

BUTTONED-UP
page 65
♥ *Jenean Morrison*

PAPER HEARTS
page 68
❤ Tula Pink

WESTMINSTER BACKPACK
page 74
❤ Ty Pennington

SWEET SIXTEEN SKIRT
page 79
❤ Kay Whitt

LOVE LETTERS QUILT
page 86
❤ Sweetwater

DRAWSTRING DRESS
page 90
❤ Amy Butler

TARGET PRACTICE BELT
page 96
❤ Anna Maria Horner

QUEEN OF HEARTS
page 99
❤ Marcia Harmening

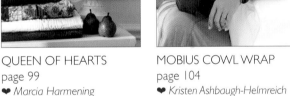

MOBIUS COWL WRAP
page 104
❤ Kristen Ashbaugh-Helmreich

TIDES COMING IN
page 106
❤ Mark Cesarik

SONOMA PURSE
page 109
❤ Patty Young

JEWELRY CASE
page 113
❤ Saremy Duffy

PETAL DRESS
page 119
❤ Anna Cohen

For instructions to make this mod patchwork heart pincushion, see page 142.

On behalf of the National Heart, Lung, and Blood Institute's *The Heart Truth*® campaign, we are proud to partner with Jimmy Beans Wool and its inspirational Stitch Red campaign. Stitch Red's mission is to spread awareness about women's heart health and to encourage women to take action to lower their risks for heart disease, one stitch at a time.

Looking to send out a personal and urgent wake-up call, *The Heart Truth*'s® main goal is to bring attention to women's personal heart health and the potential risk for heart disease. While *The Heart Truth*'s® message is geared toward women between the ages of 40 and 60, it's never too early for women to understand their risk factors. We encourage all women to be aware of the dangers of heart disease and take preventative measures to reduce their risk.

We hope you will share *The Heart Truth*'s® message with your friends and family—be aware of your risk for heart disease, get the facts about how you can take control of your heart health, and start incorporating heart-healthy behaviors into your daily routine. Remember, it is never too early or too late to take action in preventing and controlling the risk factors of heart disease.

We thank you for your continued support!

Ann M. Taubenheim, Ph.D., M.S.N.
Director
Chief, Health Campaigns
& Consumer Services Branch
National Institutes of Health, National Heart, Lung, and Blood Institute

Sewing for good

Ever dream about being on television? Well, I got *my* television career thanks to my sewing machine. Yup—if it weren't for my trusty machine and lots of homemade outfits, the possibility of a career in TV would have never occurred to me.

For as long as I can remember, I've always been making something. I graduated from making clothes for my Barbie dolls to making clothes for myself. During my senior year in high school, I had a chance to enter a contest in which you could win scholarship money for college. Unfortunately, you had to have a talent. I was too scared to sing before a crowd and too clumsy to dance, and playing an instrument was out of the question. But—I could sew. So, my cousin took lots of photos of me in my homemade outfits, I put on a combination slide show/fashion show, and holy smokes! I won.

I ended up representing Georgia at the America's Junior Miss Pageant, and while I didn't win I saw how hard the television production team worked and how much they enjoyed it. "I," I declared, "will work in television." Sewing gave me my career.

Sewing might *not* give you a career, but what it will do is give you a sense of accomplishment, help lower your blood pressure and de-stress you, and give you a way to make gifts so you can give a little piece of your heart to folks you care about.

And *Sew Red* will give you some great project ideas, along with important heart-healthy tips. I found this statistic particularly alarming: Though 80 percent of women said they would call 911 if they thought someone else was having a heart attack, barely half actually call 911 if they believe they're having a heart attack themselves! The most important thing I've learned is that most heart disease is preventable, and that women can lower their risk significantly by leading a heart-healthy lifestyle.

Sew Red will raise your awareness about the risk factors of heart disease and ways to improve your heart health. Share what you learn with a woman who's important to you by sewing up one of the beautiful designs in this book and giving it as a gift, along with a note letting her know how much she means to you and asking her to take steps to take better care of herself. If you're at risk for heart disease and find it difficult to put yourself first, please know that making good choices for your health is the best way to honor those who love you. I'm sure they'd agree that the greatest gift you can give them is to live your life to the fullest, for as long as possible.

Happy stitching! ❤
    Deborah Norville

Stick it to heart disease
one sewing project at a time!

Thank you once again for joining Jimmy Beans Wool and all of our friends in the quilting and sewing world as we "Stick It to Heart Disease" through our Stitch Red campaign to educate the public about women's heart disease! We are beyond proud of this, our newest book—*Sew Red*—and humbled by the caliber of people who devoted their time, energy, and boundless creativity to its pages. To everyone involved, thank you!

After the tremendous success of our first book in the Stitch Red campaign, *Knit Red*, we approached some of the biggest names in the sewing and quilting worlds and asked them to design projects and share their personal heart disease experiences and tips for healthy living in a new book. We were overwhelmed by the heartfelt and enthusiastic response we got, and by the beautiful projects these renowned craftspeople created for *Sew Red*.

Our Stitch Red heart-healthy campaign began with a conversation I had with my friend Marta McGinnis back in 2007. An otherwise healthy marketing executive turned sales rep who was barely in her fifties, Marta had recently survived a major heart attack and was subsequently diagnosed with heart disease. That same year my husband, Doug, an active thirty-something, was diagnosed with high blood pressure. Our shared experiences taught us that heart disease doesn't just affect older men. We were shocked to learn that heart disease is the number-one killer of women in the United States and actually kills more American women than all other diseases combined. As Marta and I talked, we realized that we needed to do something to raise awareness about this truly alarming trend. Tragically, Marta passed away just six months after that first meeting. Without her enthusiasm, the Stitch Red campaign would never have gotten off the ground. For you, Marta, and for all of those who have generously supported the campaign, thank you.

Stitch Red would never have come to life without the dedicated partnerships between Jimmy Beans Wool™ and dozens of other companies in the needle arts industry. Participating companies developed products specifically for Stitch Red and generously donate a portion of the proceeds from sales of these products to *The Heart Truth*®, an initiative of the National Heart, Lung, and Blood Institute at the National Institutes of Health.

We thank you for supporting the Stitch Red campaign through *Sew Red* and hope you will be inspired to make your own life more heart healthy.

Love ❤,
  Laura Zander (AKA Jimmy)

❤ ACKNOWLEDGMENTS

From the heart

The creation of *Sew Red* has been an adventure to say the least, and I am so grateful to all the people who have helped make this book a reality. I would also like to convey my gratitude once more to everyone who was a part of *Knit Red*, the inspiration for *Sew Red*. It was the enthusiasm and passion with which designers, yarn companies, Jimmy Beans employees, and customers alike responded to our first book that gave us the momentum to publish this one.

I would like to give a special thanks to the following individuals who were essential to my sanity throughout the process of bringing *Sew Red* to life. If it had not been for them, this book would still be an idea caught in publishing purgatory.

Nancy Jewell of Westminster Fabrics, for believing in this project from the very beginning and for introducing us to so many wonderful members of the sewing community. Your faith in us was so strong it convinced over half our contributors to sign on, resulting in a lineup of designers that surpassed our every expectation.

Amy Butler, for your unwavering support. Not only were you the first to sign on, but in addition to contributing a design, you graciously dedicated your own time and energy to making this book the best it could be.

Casey Gans of Jimmy Beans Wool, for being the Jill-of-all-trades: writing, managing, organizing—you had your finger on the pulse of every part of *Sew Red*. Your willingness to adapt at a moment's notice to the many ups, downs, and every-which-ways during this project was invaluable to its success.

John Laurie, President of Coats and Clark, North America, for your seemingly infinite confidence in me and for being an exceptional mentor. Were it not for your unending encouragement, I never would have had the guts to enter the sewing world in the first place. (And, along the same lines, a special thanks to Mike Roberts.)

Trisha Malcolm and Joy Aquilino of Sixth&Spring Books, for EVERYTHING. I admire you both beyond belief and am forever grateful for our relationship! And to Diane Lamphron, for her outstanding art direction of the photography and book design—*Sew Red* looks absolutely amazing because of you.

I would also like to express my gratitude to the designers. Thank you for listening, for your time and energy, and for believing that together, we can make a difference in the lives of our fellow crafters and the world. And most of all, thank you for selflessly jumping on board this project with almost no notice (and no idea of what you were getting yourself into)!

Finally, I would like to sincerely thank the Jimmy Beans Wool family—the gals and guys I have the privilege of working with every day, and our fabulous customers who share our love of yarn and fabric. Your unconditional support for this book, as well as my many projects, past, present, and future, means the world to me. It goes without saying that without you, Jimmy Beans Wool would not exist.

Projects and profiles

Hop! Skip! Jump!

No need to worry about cutting straight lines here! The slight waves from cutting are part of what gives this quilt charm. It's fun—and fast—to make.

FINISHED DIMENSIONS
Approximately 42½" wide × 48½" long

FABRIC
- 2 yards of 40"-wide muslin for the Foundation Blocks
- 13 assorted ¼-yard pieces of red cotton fabrics (sample uses nine prints and four solids. See Fabric Notes, below, for more details)
- 1¼ yard solid ivory cotton fabric
- 3⅓ yards blue cotton fabric for the Backing (sample shown in Haviland Blue, an RJR Fabrics *Cotton Supreme Solid*)
- ⅓ yard of red cotton fabric for the Binding

FABRIC NOTES
If you are using assorted red scraps for this quilt, you'll need approximately 50 strips that are at least 18" long and 1½" to 3½" wide.

The prints used in the sample include fabrics from Denyse's Chicopee, Flea Market Fancy, and Greenfield Hill collections for FreeSpirit Fabrics, and fabrics from DS Quilts Collection's Daisy Mae and Aunt Edna collections for Fabric Traditions. Solid fabrics used include Robert Kaufman *Kona* solids Red and Ivory, FreeSpirit Designer Solids Scarlet, and Kaffe Fassett Shot Cotton in Scarlet.

Yardages are based on 45"-wide fabric; adjust as needed.

SUPPLIES
- General Sewing Supplies (page 138)
- 50" × 60" piece of cotton batting (low loft used in sample)
- 1 spool coordinating all-purpose thread
- Rotary cutter and cutting mat
- 24" clear acrylic ruler

CUTTING THE FABRIC
1. MUSLIN
Cut three 23" × width of fabric strips; then sub-cut a total of eight 14" × 23" Foundation Blocks.

2. ASSORTED RED PRINTS AND SOLIDS
Cut a total of (50 to 55) 16" strips, each 1½" to 3½" wide. If you're using yardage, cut two 16"-long pieces from each ¼ yard, then cut the strips as illustrated in Figure 1. The quilt as shown uses 5 to 6 strips from each fabric. Place the fabric strips in three stacks: skinny, average, and wide.

3. IVORY SOLID
Cut three 16" × width of fabric strips; then sub-cut 50 to 55 pieces, each 1½" to 3½" wide. Cut pieces similar to those shown in Figure 1, using only your rotary cutter.

4. BINDING
Cut five 2½" × width of fabric strips.

TIP
Avoid using your acrylic ruler. Instead, use only your rotary cutter and don't worry about cutting perfectly straight strips. Without even trying, you will naturally cut some strips with a slight wave, and some that are somewhat straight. These slight imperfections are what give improvisational piecing its characteristic style. Avoid forcing it, however, as anything too wavy will be difficult to piece.

DENYSE SCHMIDT
Ten years ago Denyse patchworked her many experiences into one business: Denyse Schmidt Quilts. Raised by a furniture-maker father and a mother who made clothes, Denyse clearly inherited their creative genes! It was love at first sight the moment we saw Denyse's Flea Market Fancy collection, and we've been enamored with her whimsical designs ever since. Like so many, Denyse is familiar with heart disease. Her father suffered from heart issues involving his carotid artery and her sister has been diagnosed with Marfan syndrome (a connective-tissue disorder most often found in the heart). Her interest in raising awareness for her family and others was what motivated her to join us in *Sew Red*.

◆ **DENYSE'S TIP**
Hitting the gym, doing yoga, and square-dancing!

Figure 1

Figure 2

> **TIP**
> Don't worry if the edges of the pieces do not line up perfectly when placed right sides together. Focus on the small portion of fabric right in front of your needle, keeping the raw edges aligned. Pause and align the fabric as you sew down the strip. Ironing will help the piece lie flat. Steam if necessary.

Figure 3

SEWING INSTRUCTIONS

All seams are sewn right sides together using a ¼" seam allowance unless otherwise indicated. Backstitch at the beginning and end of each seam.

This Quilt Top is constructed using foundation piecing. You'll sew your ivory and red strips to a muslin block, which acts as the foundation. Two muslin foundation blocks make up each row of the quilt.

1. Begin by placing a red strip right side up on the edge of the muslin. Be sure the strip overhangs the top, bottom, and side of the muslin, as shown in Figure 2. You'll trim away the excess fabric later. Pin or staystitch the piece in place.

2. Place an ivory strip, right sides together, with the red strip. Sew through all layers, using a ¼" seam. (Figure 2) Press to set seam, then turn the red strip right side up and press again.

3. Continue alternating red and ivory strips. Your quilt will be more visually pleasing if you vary the width of your strips. (Figure 3) As you add strips, be sure your block isn't starting to distort, or curve to one side. If it is, try alternating stitch direction—rotate your block 180 degrees and stitch with the raw edges to the left of your needle.

4. Repeat steps 1 to 3 to complete all six of the foundation blocks. Begin some foundation blocks with ivory strips.

> **TIP**
> Each row is made of two foundation blocks. In each row, take care to occasionally end one block and begin the next block using the same fabric, as shown in Figure 4. This "hides" the center block seam in each row.

5. Turn over the foundation blocks and trim each to 13" wide x 22½" long.

6. Arrange your rows, rotating the blocks as needed to achieve a pleasing balance of color and pattern. Sew two foundation blocks right sides together along the short side to make a row. Set seams and press open. Repeat to make four rows. (Figure 4)

7. Pin and sew rows, right sides together, backstitching at each end. Set seams and press open.

8. With right sides together, stitch the five Binding strips together at their short ends, forming one long strip; press the strip in half lengthwise, with wrong sides together.

9. Lay the Backing wrong side up and place the batting on top, with raw edges aligned. Center the Quilt Top, right side up, on top of the batting, and secure all layers together by basting or with safety pins.

10. Quilt as desired; trim all edges even. Apply the Binding (page 141) around the perimeter of the wall hanging. ❤

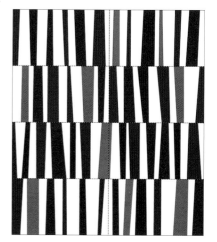

Figure 4

Spiral Scarf

Here's a little sewing magic: turn a rectangle of fabric into a bias scarf. This sleight of hand is accomplished by using a clever folding technique while sewing. The result is a classic, drapable scarf.

FINISHED DIMENSIONS
72" × 4½"

FABRICS
Nancy used rayon fabrics from her own fabric closet to make this scarf, but we recommend the following:

• ⅜ yard 44"-wide woven fabric (A) for main focal fabric (*Jenaveve Linen Pebbles* in Merlot from Valori Wells)
• ¼ yard 44"-wide complementary or contrasting woven fabric of same weight as focal fabric for the accent strip (B) (*Summersville Bella Solids* in Christmas Red from Lucie Summers)

SUPPLIES
• General Sewing Supplies (page 138)
• Matching all-purpose thread

CUTTING THE FABRIC
1. Cut two strips 6¼" wide (lengthwise grain) × 44" long (crosswise grain) from the focal fabric (A).

2. Cut two strips 2¼" wide (lengthwise grain) × 44" long (crosswise grain) from the accent fabric (B).

SEWING INSTRUCTIONS
Sew all seams with right sides together, using a ¼" seam allowance, unless otherwise indicated. Backstitch at the beginning and end of each seam.

1. Pin and stitch (or serge) the two accent strips (B) at one short end with a ¼" seam allowance. Repeat for the two strips of focal fabric (A). Press the seams open.

2. Pin and stitch (or serge) the focal fabric (A) to the accent fabric (B) along one long (44") edge with a ¼" seam allowance, forming a rectangle. Press the seam open.

3. Measure and trim the rectangle to exactly 8" × 80".
Note from Nancy: In order for the sewing magic to happen (i.e., for the rectangle to turn into a bias scarf) the length must be evenly divisible by the width. Sound difficult? It's not tricky as long as the rectangle is exactly 8" × 80".

4. With right sides together, fold one corner of the rectangle to meet the opposite long edge of the rectangle; pin. Mark ¼" up from the bottom raw edge of the folded triangle. (Figure 1)

5. Begin stitching at the upper folded tip with a ¼" seam allowance. Stitch along the cut edges, stopping with the needle down in the fabric at the ¼" mark (i.e., ¼" before raw edge of the folded-over corner). Keep the needle down in the fabric. (Figure 2)

6. With the needle still down in the fabric, raise the presser foot. Take the bottom raw edge of the folded corner and pivot it up until

NANCY ZIEMAN
Nancy is the host and executive producer of *Sewing with Nancy*, the longest-running sewing and quilting program on televison: It's been on the air for more than 30 years! Nancy is now a sewing and quilting guru who, luckily for us, made time in her busy schedule to design for *Sew Red*. We couldn't be happier to have her expertise. Before Nancy gets into her daily design and filming groove, she visits her local Larsen, Wisconsin, YMCA for an early morning swim. Once her workout is out of the way, she is better focused for work. And although many of us are taught that staying heart-healthy means avoiding all things sugary and sweet, Nancy thinks that life does not have to be so restrictive, and does not deprive herself of desserts. Balance and moderation are the keys for her.

NANCY'S TIP
Do you have a sweet tooth that gives you trouble? Take one "polite bite" of dessert so you can appease that overbearing sweet tooth, but not feel guilty for overdoing it.

it meets the long (80") raw edge of the rectangle. The fabric will begin to spiral. (Figure 3)

7. Lower the presser foot; continue to stitch the seam down the length, pulling the raw edge of the top fabric over to meet the raw edge of the bottom fabric. (Figure 4)

8. Stop stitching at approximately half the length of the scarf; backstitch to secure stitching. Leave a gap of about 6 inches, then continue to pin the raw edges of the fabric strip together. (Figure 5)

9. Raise the presser foot and clip the thread tails. Advance the presser foot to the next pin, leaving the 6" length of the seam unstitched. (This unstitched 6" gap is for turning the scarf right side out in step 13.)

10. Beginning after the 6" gap, pin and continue stitching the seam until nearing the end of the lower layer of fabric. (Figure 6) Place a pin ¼ from the lower layer's corner and stop stitching at that pin marking. (Figure 7)

11. Raise the presser foot, pivot the raw edge of the upper layer of fabric to match its remaining raw edge to the raw edge of the lower layer of fabric, forming a folded corner/triangle as you did in step 4. (Figure 8) Stitch to the point. (Figure 9)

12. Press the seams open.
Note from Nancy: Insert a wooden dowel into the scarf opening. Press over the dowel, which will make it easy to press the spiraling seam.

13. Turn the scarf right side out through the opening. (Figure 10) Hand stitch the opening closed. ♥

TIP
This scarf can be even faster to sew! Choose one fabric— ½ yard— and cut two 8" crosswise strips. Seam the two strips together along one short end. Then, follow steps 3–4.

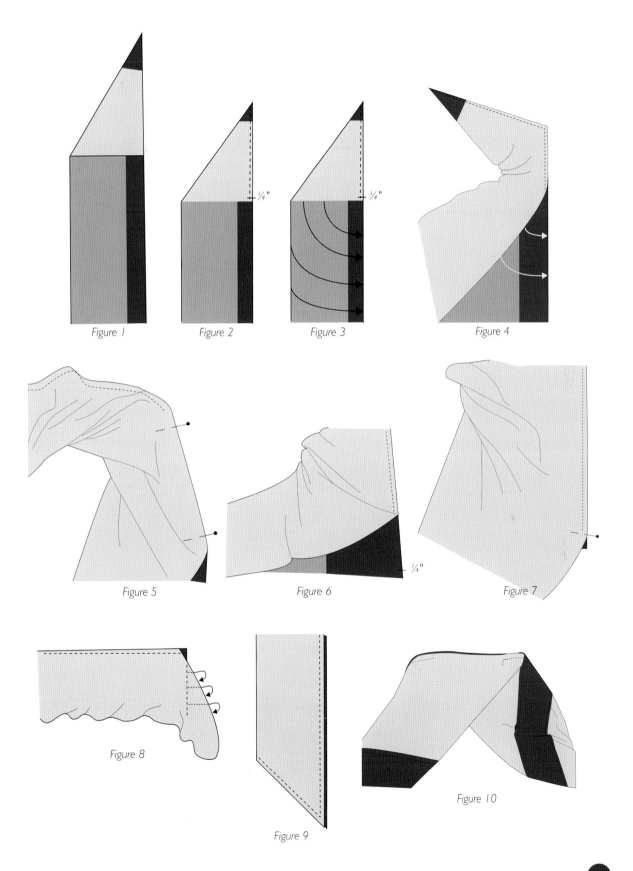

Figure 1

Figure 2

¼"

Figure 3

¼"

Figure 4

Figure 5

Figure 6

¼"

Figure 7

Figure 8

Figure 9

Figure 10

 **ANEELA HOEY**

Snowball Table Runner

Two beloved quilting blocks, snowball and four patch, team up in this fun-to-sew table runner. Create a whimsical runner reminiscent of folktales and childhood play.

ANEELA HOEY
Both a quilter and embroiderer, Aneela is quite the crafty creator. Her fabric collection, *A Walk in the Woods* (which we so fondly refer to as "little red"), is among our favorites. We couldn't be happier to have one of Aneela's imaginative quilts in *Sew Red*. At 41, she is in good heart health, and while she keeps a busy schedule sewing, quilting, embroidering, knitting, and raising her two daughters, Aneela still manages to get in her daily exercise—walking her daughters to and from school each day, a total of six miles round trip. When she is home, Aneela keeps herself busy doing things she loves, which in turn keeps her from snacking. She wouldn't want to get crumbs or drips on her fabrics.

FINISHED DIMENSIONS
16" x 37"

FABRIC
- Twenty 4" x 4" red print squares of quilting cotton (all print fabrics used in the sample are from the *Sherbet Pips*, *Little Apples*, *A Walk in the Woods*, and *Sew Stitchy* collections, all by Aneela Hoey for Moda Fabrics)
- Twenty 4" x 4" white/red print squares (fabrics as above)
- ⅜ yard solid white fabric (A) for the Snowball Corners and Sashing (*Moda Bella* solid in White Bleached used in the sample)
- ½ yard coordinating fabric (B) for the Backing (*Leaves in Lollipop* from the *Little Apples* collection by Aneela Hoey used in the sample)
- ¼ yard coordinating fabric (C) for the Binding (*Skipping Square Dots* in Cherry

from the *Sherbet Pips* collection by Aneela Hoey used in the sample)

SUPPLIES
- General Sewing Supplies (page 138)
- 18" x 40" piece of batting
- 24"-long ruler or yardstick
- White cotton sewing thread (Aurifil 50wt in white 2024 used in the sample)
- Red cotton sewing thread (Aurifil 28wt in red 1103 used in the sample)
- 2"-wide masking tape
- Bent arm quilting pins

CUTTING THE FABRIC
1. SOLID WHITE (A)
Cut two 2" x 40" strips; cut each strip into twenty 2" squares for a total of 40 squares for the Snowball Corners.
Cut two 1½" x 40" strips and two 1½" x 20" strips for the Sashing.

2. BINDING (C)
Cut three strips 2½" x 110".

 ANEELA'S TIP
Eat porridge for breakfast! This delicious morning meal is essential to starting your day off right, and eating whole-grain-rich porridge will give you energy to stay full all morning.

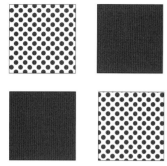

Figure 1

Figure 2

Figure 3

Figure 4

SEWING INSTRUCTIONS

All seams are sewn right sides together, with ¼" seam allowances, unless otherwise indicated.

PIECING THE BLOCKS

1. Take 2 red print squares and 2 white-and-red print squares and arrange them into a four-patch block so that the red prints are diagonally opposite from each other and the white-and-red prints are also diagonally opposite. (Figure 1)

2. Place the top two squares right sides together and stitch. Repeat with the bottom two squares; press the seams open.

3. Place the two pieced strips right sides together and stitch. Press the seams open. (Figure 2)

4. Draw a diagonal line from corner to corner on the wrong side of each of the white 2" squares. (Figure 3)

5. With right sides together, place a white 2" square at one of the corners of the pieced four-patch block. Stitch them together by sewing along the drawn line on the wrong side of the white square. (Figure 3)

6. Repeat step 5 on the remaining 3 corners of the pieced four-patch block. Trim the excess seam allowance at each corner ¼" from the drawn pencil lines on the white squares. (Figure 3)

7. Press the seams toward the patchwork to make the finished block. Repeat steps 1–6 to make a total of 10 blocks. (Figure 4)

MAKING THE TABLE RUNNER FRONT

8. Arrange the 10 blocks into 2 rows of 5 blocks each; sew each row of 5 blocks together. Press the seams open.

9. Join the top and bottom rows from step 8 together and press the seams open again to form the patchwork Centerpiece.

10. Stitch one of the 1½" × 40" Sashing strips to the top long edge of the patchwork Centerpiece and the other Sashing to the bottom long edge of the Centerpiece. Press the seams open; trim the side edges of the Centerpiece even.

11. Sew one of the 1½" × 20" Sashing strips to each short side of the Centerpiece. Press the seams open and trim the top and bottom edges of the Centerpieces even. This is your Table Runner Front.

QUILTING THE TABLE RUNNER

12. Press the Backing fabric (B) and place it wrong side up onto the floor or on a large table. Place the batting on top, aligning the edges with the Backing fabric underneath.

13. Center the Table Runner Front on top of the batting, right side up; the batting is sandwiched between the Backing and the Front. Secure the 3 layers of the table runner together using bent arm safety pins.

14. Quilt as you wish, removing pins as you go. (I used an machine embroidery stitch on my sewing machine, a Pfaff quilt expression 4.0, for my sample.)

15. Trim the side edges even using a rotary cutter, ruler, and cutting mat.

ATTACHING THE BINDING

16. Take 2 Binding strips, place them right sides together, and stitch along one of the short ends to join them. Stitch the third Binding strip to the pieced strip in the same way; press the seams open.

17. With wrong sides together, fold the Binding strip in half lengthwise; press. Attach the Binding to the table runner (pages 140–141). ♥

You Are So Loved

What better Valentine's Day gift could there be than a warm quilt that evokes old-fashioned valentines with a declaration of love?

QUILTED BY DARLA PADILLA

FINISHED DIMENSIONS
40" × 42"

FABRIC
- 1 yard of white quilting cotton (A) for the Center Block (Bella *Solid White* in the sample)
- ⅜ yard of small red polka dot quilting cotton (B) for the Appliqué Letters and Red Inner Border (*8654-52 Essential Dots* in Christmas Red used for the sample)
- 2 yards of large red and white polka dot fabric (C) for the Outer Border and the Backing (Dottie White *Christmas Red 45008 11* used in the sample)
- ½ yard solid red fabric (D) for the Binding (Bella Solids *Christmas Red 9900* 16 used in the sample)

All fabrics used in the sample are by Moda. Yardages are based on 45"-wide fabric; adjust as needed.

SUPPLIES
- General Sewing Supplies (page 138)
- Matching all-purpose thread
- Paper-backed fusible web
- Safety pins (optional)

CUTTING THE FABRIC

1. From white fabric A, cut one 34" × 35" rectangle.

2. From the Outer Border fabric C, cut four 2"-wide Outer Border strips, two 37" long and two 39" long.

3. From the Inner Border and Appliqué Letters fabric B, cut four 1½"-wide strips, two 35" long and two 36" long, for the Inside Border. Use the rest of Fabric B for the letters.

4. From the Backing fabric C, cut a 40" × 40" square.

6. Cut three 2¼" × width of the fabric strips from fabric D for the Binding.

VANESSA CHRISTENSON
We feel very lucky to have found Vanessa, a 36-year-old quilter, wife, and mother of four from San Diego who runs V & Co., a shop that sells quilting and sewing patterns for home accessories, clothing, and bags. We wondered how Vanessa stays in such great shape while simultaneously running a store and tending to her family. Her answer? Get up bright and early (before the husband and kids!) and go for a 4½-mile walk. Vanessa also likes to keep her family physically active and turns things like trips to the ice cream shop into a stroll around the neighborhood or a family bike ride. We love hearing stories about how families teach their little ones to live healthy lifestyles!

♥ **VANESSA'S TIP**
Work out with your buddies! Exercising in a group makes it very hard to miss a workout because your friends (who will rarely take no for an answer) will call and text until you get out the door.

TRACING AND CUTTING THE LETTERS

The Appliqué Letters Template is on a pattern sheet included with this book.

5. Using the templates and a pencil, trace the Appliqué Letters onto the paper side of the fusible web. Trace the words "you are so loved" (you'll need to trace the "o" three times). Your letters will be backwards when you trace them.

6. Cut out the traced letters at least ⅛" outside the traced lines.

7. Place the letters on the wrong side of the Appliqué Letters fabric (B).

8. Iron the letters onto fabric B following the manufacturer's instructions.

9. Cut out the letters on the traced lines.

SEWING INSTRUCTIONS

All seams are sewn right sides together using a ¼" seam allowance unless otherwise noted.

1. Lay the 34" × 35" Center Block rectangle (fabric A) right side up and measure 3" from the bottom edge and 4" in from the right edge of the Block; mark both positions.

2. Remove the paper backing from the wrong side of each letter.

3. Place the word "loved" right side up at the marks from step 1, 3" up from the bottom edge and 4" in from the right edge.

4. Center the words "are so" ½" above the top of the letters "l" and "d" in the word "loved." Center the word "you" ½" above the words "are so."

5. Pin all the words in place and fuse them in position to the Center Block following the manufacturer's instructions. Alternatively, you can zigzag or straight stitch around the outside of the letters to attach them to the Center Block.

6. With right sides together, pin the two 1½" × 35" Inner Border strips (B) to the left and right edges of the Center Block and the two 1½" × 36" Inner Border strips to the top and bottom of the Center Block. Stitch all seams, then press them flat.

7. With right sides together, pin the two 2" × 36" Outer Border strips (C) to the Inner Border strips on the sides of the Quilt Block and the two 2" × 39" Outer Border strips to the Inner Border strips at the top and bottom of the Quilt Block. Stitch all seams, then press them flat to complete the Quilt Top.

10. Lay the Backing piece (D) wrong side up and place the batting on top, with raw edges aligned. Center the Quilt Top, right side up, on top of the batting, and secure all layers together by basting or with safety pins.

11. Quilt as desired; trim all edges even.

12. With right sides together, stitch the three Binding strips (D) together at their short ends, forming one long strip; press the strip in half lengthwise, with wrong sides together. Apply the Binding (page 141) around the perimeter of the quilt. ❤

 **KAARI MENG**

Chateau Necklace

This easy-to-make beaded necklace can be worked with scraps of cotton quilting fabric. The dainty flower detail is a stack of fabric circles secured with a button and a ribbon.

KAARI MENG
Kaari is the mastermind behind French General Textiles, Notions & Vintage Crafts. Over a glass of heart-healthy red wine, Laura asked her to design a project for *Sew Red* and she immediately said, "I'm in!" Every summer for the past 22 years, Kaari has taken groups of women to a chateau in France for workshops on sewing, stitching, paper crafts, and jewelry making, plus day trips to flea markets, farmers markets, and local artisans. In fact, Amy Butler is joining the France (and Bath!) excursion, on which the group has been invited to stay at a duke's house complete with King Henry VIII and Jane Seymour's wedding bed! While Kaari does not deny herself some goodies like croissants, cheese, and foie gras on these trips, she's also picked up many healthy French eating habits, like small portions and fresh, local food.

FINISHED DIMENSIONS
Necklace is as long as desired. The necklace shown uses 42 stuffed beads for a total length of about 44"; make more or fewer beads to make a different length necklace as desired.

FABRIC
• Assorted scraps of cotton quilting-weight fabric to cut forty-two 2½" circles
• A Moda Candy pack, which has forty-two 2½" squares (Chateau Rouge by French General, Fall 2012, used in the sample)
• Extra scrap fabric for the flower

SUPPLIES
• General Sewing Supplies (page 138)
• 1 decorative button
• ½ yard of ¼"-wide ribbon
• Cotton batting
• All-purpose thread
• Paper (for pattern)
• Pencil
• Pencil compass
• Knitting needle or chopstick

CUTTING THE FABRIC
1. On paper, use a compass to draw a 2½"-diameter circle to make a pattern for the stuffed beads (seam allowance is included); cut out the pattern.

2. Trace the pattern onto the fabric scraps and cut out.

3. Cut 6 more circles from the extra scrap fabric for the flower. Set one circle aside, and then trim the edges of the remaining 5 circles so each is progressively smaller, with the smallest circle being 1" in diameter.

SEWING INSTRUCTIONS
MAKING A BEAD
(This starts with the same process as making a quilter's yoyo.)

1. With your fingers, lightly press the edge of the circle under ¼" (toward the wrong side of your fabric).

2. With a hand-sewing needle and thread, sew a running stitch (using even stitches about ⅛" long) around the edge of the circle through both layers of fabric, ⅛" from the folded edge.

❤ **KAARI'S TIP**
Don't deny yourself any goodies (like foie gras); just keep portion size in mind and stick with fresh foods.

3. Pull the thread slightly to gather the stitches, pulling the circle's edge in toward the center and leaving enough space to insert batting. Leave the needle on the thread and don't cut the thread ends.

4. Working with small pinches of batting at a time, firmly stuff the circle. Use a knitting needle or chopstick to push the batting into the opening. Shape the bead with your fingers a bit to achieve the desired look.

5. Pull the thread to close the opening completely. Make a small stitch at the opening and pass the needle through the stitch loop, then pull the stitch tight. (Don't worry if there's a tiny hole; you'll sew that up in the next step.)

6. With the smallest stitch possible, stitch back and forth across the hole a few times to completely close it. Tie off the thread and trim the ends.

7. Repeat steps 1 to 6 to make 42 beads.

FINISHING THE NECKLACE

8. Sew the beads to each other by making several small stitches through the side of each bead, pulling the stitches tight and keeping the gathered sides of the beads all facing in the same direction. Cut the thread and tie the ends together after joining each bead. Make the joining stitches on the exact opposite sides of each bead so they hang in a straight line.

9. Connect all the beads in this manner to form a loop.

10. To make the flower, stack the flower circles right side up with the smallest on top. Hand-stitch through the center several times, then sew the button to the top of the flower; do not cut the thread.

11. Tie the ribbon in a bow; hand-stitch the bow to the back of the flower.

12. Sew the flower to the top of one bead, opposite the gathered side. Stitch all the way through the bead to keep the flower from drooping. Tie off the stitching on the gathered side of the bead and trim the thread ends. ♥

Asian Modern Pillow

Scraps of silk kimono fabric are hand cut, layered, and appliquéd at odd angles like an abstract expressionist's cityscape. This pillow makes a modern statement in any room.

FINISHED DIMENSIONS
20" × 20"

FABRIC
- ⅝ yard of a main fabric of your choice (A) for Front Background and pillow Back (a red silk ikat from Linda's personal collection used in the sample)
- ⅝ yard of a contrast print fabric (B) for Feature Strip (black-and-white cotton ikat from Linda's personal collection used in the sample)
- ½ yard (or one fat quarter) of check or plaid fabric (C) for the flat Piping (black-and-white silk dupioni from Linda's personal collection used in the sample)
- 7 to 9 small scraps of silk print fabrics for layered Appliques (silk kimono fabrics from Linda's personal collection used in the sample)

SUPPLIES
- General Sewing Supplies (page 138)
- 1 skein embroidery floss for sashiko stitching
- 1 spool 100% cotton sewing thread, to match base fabric
- Hand sewing needles for embroidery floss and regular thread weight
- Rotary cutter
- Straight edge ruler
- 20" × 20" down and feather pillow form
- Fusible web tape

♥ **TIP**
Here are two places to find vintage Japanese (and similar) fabrics: *www.saberdesigns.cc* and *www.bohemianelement. com*

CUTTING THE FABRIC
½" seam allowances are included in the following cutting measurements, based on using a down and feather pillow form. If you are using a polyester fill pillow form, add ½" to the following cutting measurements.

1. BASE FABRIC A
Cut one 13½" (crosswise grain) × 20" (lengthwise grain) for the pillow front. Cut one 20" × 20" for the pillow back.

2. CONTRAST FABRIC B
Cut one 7½" (crosswise grain) × 20" (lengthwise grain) for the feature strip.

LINDA LEE
Linda started her design career in the 6th grade by making and selling felt hats. She clearly had a brain for business, because that small beginning forecasted a life-long career designing creative sewing patterns for the adventurous sewer. We find it fitting that she's re-created the fabulous pillow design that launched her career and brought fame to her doorstep for this book. As a past local chairwoman for the Heart Association's annual fundraiser in Topeka, Kansas, it is no surprise that Linda jumped into *Sew Red* with great enthusiasm. The key to Linda's excellent heart health at 64 is exercise. She works out with a personal trainer a couple of times a week and is very involved in tennis, traveling anywhere she can find a good tournament! As a clothing designer, she watches her weight because she is conscious of the ever-present tape measure at her waist.

♥ **LINDA'S TIP**
Find some form of exercise you love—activity is the key to a healthy heart!

3. PIPING FABRIC C
Cut one 2" × 20" strip (on the bias grain).

4. APPLIQUÉS
Cut 7 to 9 squares and rectangles in random sizes. Use scissors to cut imperfect shapes.

SEWING INSTRUCTIONS
Sew all seams with right sides together, using a ½" seam allowance, unless otherwise indicated. Backstitch at the beginning and end of each seam.

1. Fold the bias strip in half lengthwise (wrong sides together) and press. Re-cut the strip to an even ¾" width when folded.

2. With raw edges aligned, machine baste the folded bias strip to one long edge of the Feature Strip (B), keeping the stitching an even ¼" from the bias strip's fold. (Figure 1)

3. Place the raw-edged applique pieces along the left edge of the Front Background fabric (A), arranging and overlapping them in a pleasing manner. Once the design is set, use the fusible web tape to temporarily fuse the pieces in place. Cut off the excess fabric pieces from the left edge.

4. Using three strands of embroidery floss, hand sew long running stitches to outline each raw edge of the appliqués. (Figure 2)

5. With right sides together, sew the Feature Strip to the appliquéd Front using the basting line from step 2 as a sewing guide. Press the seam toward the Feature Strip. (Figure 3)

6. Sew the prepared front to the pillow Back around all four sides, leaving an opening along the bottom edge for inserting the pillow form.

7. Turn the pillow to the right side. Insert the pillow form and slipstitch the opening closed. ♥

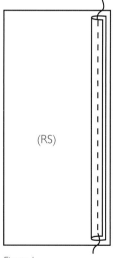

Figure 1

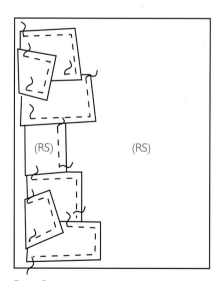

Figure 2

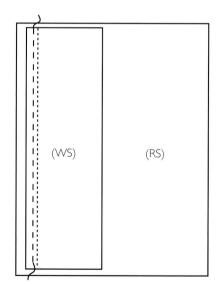

Figure 3

Pathfinder Quilt

This modern version of zigzag movement creates a pathway through the quilt. The negative space provides a great opportunity for free motion quilting.

VALORI WELLS

Valori is a professional quilter, author, and fabric and pattern designer, and she's also a mom and a co-owner of the Stitchin' Post in Sisters, Oregon. As soon as we started selling fabric at Jimmy Beans Wool, we knew we had to have her fabric and pattern collections in our inventory; they soon were among our bestsellers. Her above-garage studio is her haven, but it's close to her kitchen and the allure of her favorite snack, Cheez-Its. How does she avoid the temptation? By crafting—why waste time snacking when you can be creating a new fabric design or sewing just one more seam? To assure that her little ones grow up knowing how yummy healthy food can be, Valori cooks her family appealing, nutritious meals.

FINISHED DIMENSIONS
48½" × 76"

FABRIC
QUILTING COTTON (SOLIDS) FOR THE BACKGROUND
These gray quilting cottons are all from Free Spirit.
- 1 yard light gray (*Designer Essentials Solid Pastel Gray* used in the sample)
- 1 yard dark gray (*Designer Essentials Solid Manatee* used in the sample)
- ⅞ yard medium gray (*Designer Essentials Nugray* used in the sample)
- ⅞ yard medium dark gray (*Designer Essentials Slate Gray* used in the sample)

QUILTING COTTON (PRINTS) FOR THE ZIGZAGS
All of the print (and the solid red) fabrics are from Valori's collections for Free Spirit.
- ¼ yard each of 7 different red prints in a variety of light, medium, and dark values (*Grace* in Coral from the *Cocoon* collection, *Wild Field* in Cranberry from the *Wrenly Christmas* collection, *Bloom* in Cinnamon from the *Wrenly* collection, *Paisley* and *Chandelier*, both in Red, from the *Delhi* collection; *Poppy Centers* in Red from the *Isabella* collection, and *Designer Essentials Solid Red* used in the sample)
- ½ yard coordinating quilting cotton for Binding (*Designer Essentials Solid Red* used in the sample)
- 3 yards coordinating quilting cotton for the Backing (*Grace* in Coral from the *Cocoon* collection used in the sample)

Yardages are based on 45"-wide fabric; adjust as needed.

SUPPLIES
- General Sewing Supplies (page 138)
- 57" × 83" piece of batting
- Rotary cutter and cutting mat
- Coordinating all-purpose thread

CUTTING INSTRUCTIONS
Refer to the Assembly Diagram.
From the solid Background fabrics, cut pieces as follows:

Light gray:
A: 14⅜" square
B: 10½" square
G: 8½" × 36½" rectangle
I: 8½" × 22½" rectangle

Medium gray:
A: 14⅜" square
B: 10½" square
E: 5" × 15½" rectangle
M: 3¾" × 14½" rectangle
F: 8½" × 40½" rectangle

Medium dark gray:
A: 14⅜" square
B: 10½" square
D: 5" × 41½" rectangle

VALORI'S TIP
The mind is a very powerful tool. The more time and effort you spend making the conscious decision to live healthy, the more likely you are to create lasting healthy habits. (It's a case of mind over matter—or in this case, mind over Cheez-Its.)

ASSEMBLY DIAGRAM

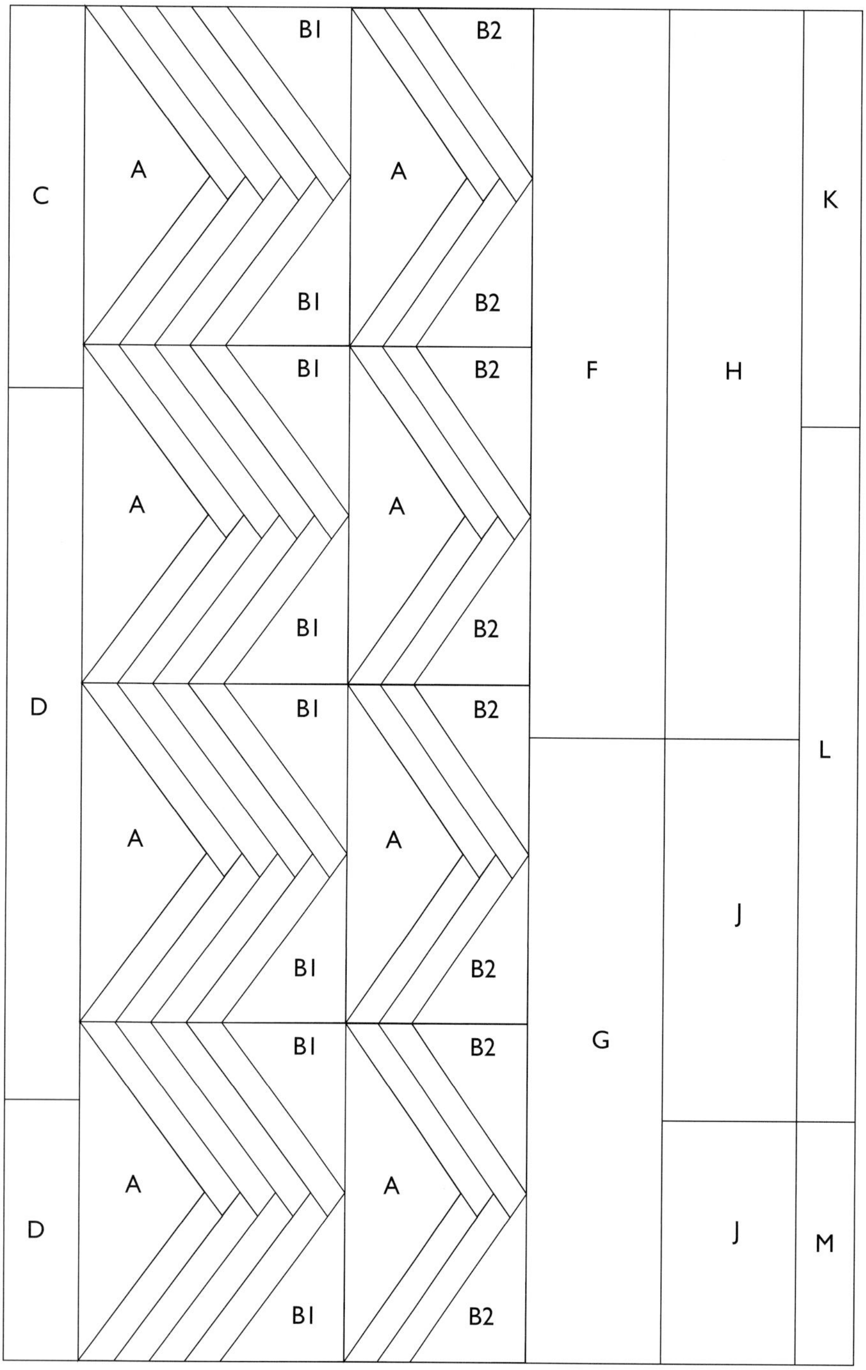

Figure 1

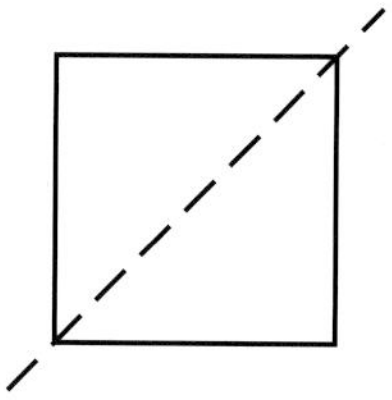

Figure 2

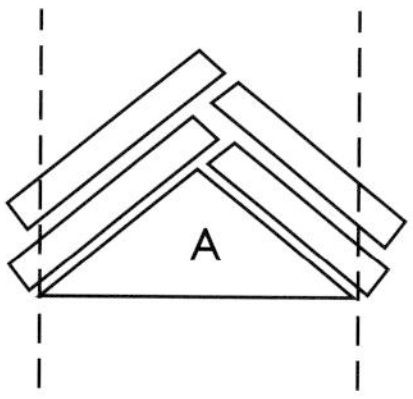

Figure 3

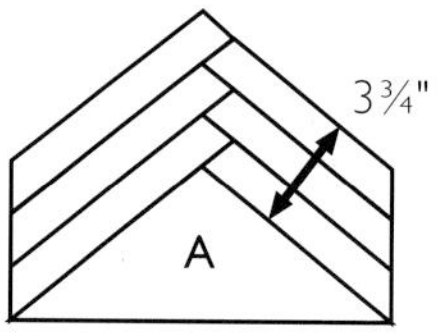

3¾"

Figure 4

B1   B1

Row 1

A

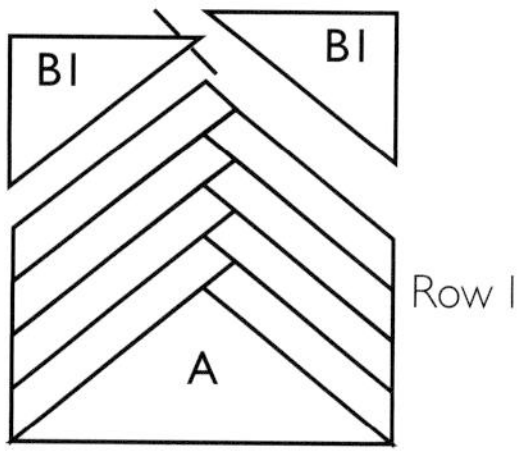

Figure 5

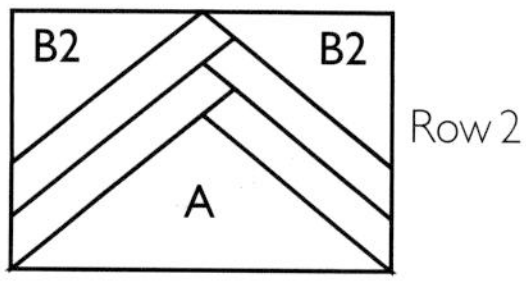

B2   B2

Row 2

A

H: 8½" × 40½" rectangle
L: 3¾" × 40½" rectangle

Dark gray
A: 14⅞" square
B: 10½" square
J: 8½" × 14½" rectangle
C: 5" × 21½" rectangle
K: 3¾" × 22½" rectangle

1. Stack the four 14⅞" squares (A) on top of each other and cut them diagonally in half from corner to corner to make 8 triangles. (Figure 1)

2. Stack the four 10½" squares (B) on top of each other and cut them diagonally in half from corner to corner in each direction to make a total of 16 triangles that are half the size of the A triangles.

3. Red Prints: Cut three or four 42"-long strips from each of the 7 red prints; cut half the strips 1" wide and half 1½" wide (cut additional strips as needed later). Use a ruler or cut the strips freehand for a more organic look if desired.

4. Cut the Backing fabric in half crosswise. Pin and stitch these pieces together to make a piece 1½ yards × twice the width of fabric.

5. Cut nine 3" × width of fabric Binding strips.

SEWING INSTRUCTIONS
All seams are sewn with right sides together using a ¼" seam allowance unless otherwise indicated. Backstitch at the beginning and end of each seam.

Refer to the Assembly Diagram.
1. Begin with the Row 2 Zigzag Blocks. Attach strips to each side of the A triangle (from Cutting step 1), beginning on the left side. (Figure 2) Press each seam flat after stitching. Add strips until the strips add up to 3¾" wide, as shown in Figure 3. Trim the sides of the strips, leaving a little extra. You will square up the block later.

2. Add a B triangle (from Cutting step 2) to the left side of block A. Trim off the point. (Figure 4) Add the B triangle to the right side of block A. (Figure 4) Press after each seam. Square up the block to 16½" × 20". Make three more blocks in the same way.

3. Construct the Row 3 Blocks in the same way but add only 2 rows of red strips before adding the B triangles. (Figure 5) Trim these blocks to 11½" × 20".

4. Lay out all of the Blocks following the Diagram. Stitch the Row 1 Blocks together; press. Stitch the Row 2 Blocks together; press. Stitch Row 1 to Row 2; press. Continue the process until the six rows are stitched together. Press to complete the Quilt Front.

5. With right sides together, stitch the Binding strips together at their short ends, forming one long strip; press the strip in half lengthwise, with wrong sides together. Trim the Binding strip to 260".

6. Lay the Backing wrong side up and place the batting on top, with raw edges aligned. Center the Quilt Front, right side up, on top of the batting, and baste or safety pin all layers together.

7. Quilt as desired. The sample was quilted in red thread in a zigzag pattern to mimic the zigzags of the quilting design, filled in with a teardrop shape, and connected together like a vine.

8. Trim all edges even. Apply the Binding (page 141) to the quilt. ❤

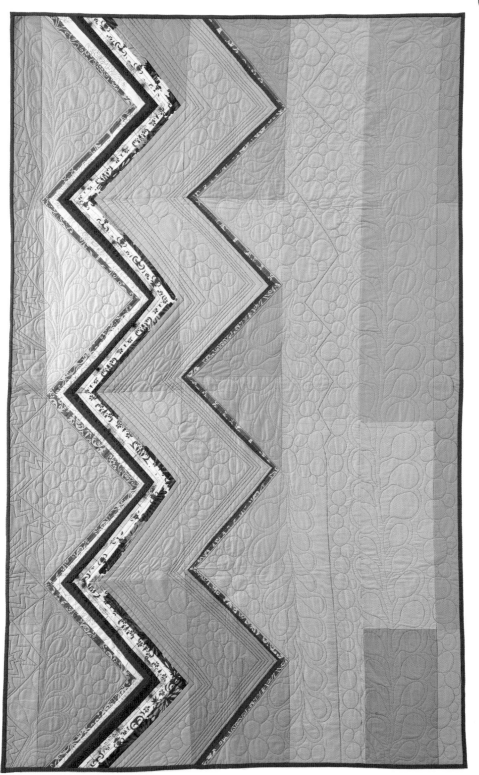

♥ Full view
of quilt

Village Bag

Polka dots, polka dots, polka dots! This adorable tote is made with four different patterned fabrics. It's quick and easy to sew, and makes a great gift for a girl of any age!

FINISHED DIMENSIONS
13" wide x 13½" long
(30" long including strap)
Tie: 2" x 18"

FABRIC
- ¾ yard fabric (A) for Exterior Bag and Handle (*Essential Dots #8654-51* by Moda used for the sample)
- ¾ yard coordinating fabric (B) for Bag Lining, Cuff Lining, and Exterior Cuff (*Redy Set Snow #22153-11* by Me and My Sister Designs for Moda used for the sample)
- ⅛ yard coordinating fabric (C) for Cuff accent strips (*Ready Set Snow #22156-11* by Me and My Sister Designs for Moda used for the sample)
- ¼ yard coordinating fabric (D) for decorative Tie (*Oh-Cherry-Oh #22096-11* by Me and My Sister Designs for Moda used for the sample)

Yardage is based on 40"-wide fabric; adjust as needed.

SUPPLIES
- General Sewing Supplies (page 138)
- 1 yard fusible fleece for interfacing (Pellon 987F used for the sample)
- Coordinating all-purpose thread

CUTTING THE FABRIC
The pattern for the Exterior Bag and Bag Lining is on a pattern sheet included with this book. Cut all pieces on the fold. The remaining pieces are cut from the measurements in the following steps.

1. FROM FABRIC A
(FOR EXTERIOR BAG AND HANDLE)
Cut two Exterior Bag pieces from Patterns A and B.
Cut one 6" x 36" strip.

2. FROM FABRIC B
(FOR BAG LINING, CUFF LINING, AND EXTERIOR CUFF)
Cut two Bag Lining pieces from Pattern A.
Cut one 4¼" x 24" rectangle for the Cuff Lining.
Cut three 1¼" x 24" strips for the Exterior Cuff.

3. FROM FABRIC C
(FOR CUFF ACCENT STRIPS)
Cut two 1¼" x 24" strips.

ME AND MY SISTER DESIGNS

These two sisters, Barbara Groves and Mary Jacobson, were hooked forever after taking their first quilting class, and soon their dreams of creating beautiful quilts turned to dreams of quilt-shop ownership. The best part of owning their own shop was creating samples, which made them realize that their true passion was designing. Their design company, Me and My Sister Designs, took off when Moda fabrics invited them to design fabrics. As a proud vendor of Moda's fabrics, we couldn't resist this adorable duo. Heart disease is close to their hearts (no pun intended)—their grandmother passed away due to heart problems from rheumatic fever and their grandfather from a heart attack. Barb and Mary have yearly checkups, keep a close eye on their blood pressure, make smart food decisions, eat small portions, and walk as frequently as they can.

♥ **BARB & MARY'S TIP**
Whatever you do, do not ruin brownies with pureed beets! (Even though some of the girls at Jimmy Beans Wool swear by it.)

4. FROM FABRIC D (FOR DECORATIVE TIE)
Cut one 8" × 20" rectangle.

5. FROM FUSIBLE FLEECE (FOR INTERFACING)
Cut two exterior bag interfacing pieces from Patterns A and B.
Cut one 6" × 36" strip for the handle.
Cut one 4¼" × 24" rectangle for the Cuff Lining.
Cut one 4¼" × 24" rectangle for the Exterior Cuff.

SEWING INSTRUCTIONS
All seams are sewn right sides together using a ¼" seam allowance unless otherwise indicated. Backstitch at the beginning and end of each seam.

1. Following the manufacturer's instructions, fuse the interfacing pieces onto the wrong side of the fabric pieces as follows: 2 Exterior Bag pieces, 1 Handle strip, and 1 Cuff Lining rectangle. The interfacing for the Exterior Cuff will be fused later, after the Cuff Exterior is pieced.

2. Place the two Exterior Bag pieces with the interfacing sides facing up. Place the pattern on top and, starting at the dots, mark four 1½"-long vertical pleat lines on the interfacing. Repeat on other Exterior Bag piece and on both Bag Lining pieces. (Figure 1)

EXTERIOR BAG AND LINING
3. Working from the wrong side, make the pleats on the front and back Exterior Bag and Lining pieces (a total of 4 pleats). Pinch the fabric between the pleat marks so that they meet; pin. Stitch from the top to the bottom of the pleat, backstitching at both ends. Press the pleats away from the center. (Figure 2)

4. Stitch the 2 Exterior Bag pieces together. Clip the curves and turn the bag right side out. Sew the Bag Lining the same way, but leave an 8" opening on the bottom seam for turning the bag in step 13. Do not turn the lining right side out. (Figure 3)

1½"

Figure 1

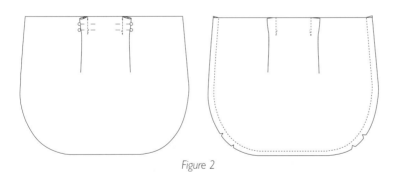

Figure 2

8"

Figure 3

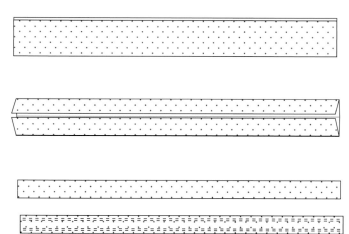

Figure 4

Figure 5

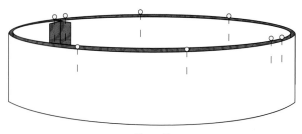

Figure 6

Figure 7

HANDLE

5. Fold the 6" × 36" Handle strip in half lengthwise with wrong sides together and press a crease down the center. Open the strip and fold both long raw edges in so that they meet along the pressed center fold; press. Refold along the center crease so that both folded outer edges meet and press. The Handle strip now measures 1½" × 36". Topstitch ¼", then ⅜", from the outer edges along the two long sides of the Handle. (Figure 4)

EXTERIOR CUFF

6. With right sides together, pin and stitch the three 1¼" × 24" Exterior Cuff strips and the two 1¼" × 24" contrasting Exterior Cuff strips together lengthwise, alternating fabrics as shown in Figure 5. Press the seam allowances open. Apply the remaining 4¼" × 24" fusible interfacing rectangle to the wrong side of the pieced Exterior Cuff.

7. With the seams aligned, sew the short ends of the pieced Exterior Cuff together using a ½" seam allowance. Press the seam allowance open. Repeat for the Cuff Lining. (Figure 6)

8. Place the Cuff Lining inside the Exterior Cuff with right sides together, matching seams and raw edges; pin. (Figure 7)

9. Measure in 5¾" from each side of the Cuff seam and mark with a pin. Slip the raw end of the Handle between the two Cuff layers and center it on the 5¾" pin mark, aligning raw edges. (Figure 8) Make sure that the Handle is not twisted. Stitch a ½" seam around the entire top.

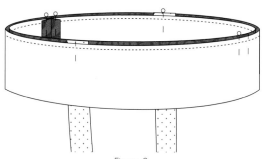

Figure 8

10. Turn the Cuff right side out and press. Machine baste ¼" away from the raw edges around the bottom of the Cuff. Topstitch close to the seam lines on both sides of the Cuff Accent strips. (Figure 9)

PUTTING IT TOGETHER

11. With right sides together, place the Handle/Cuff unit over the Exterior Bag. Align the handle ends over the side Exterior Bag seams and center the single Cuff seam between the two pleats on one of the sides. Align the raw edges and baste in place using a ¼" seam. (Figure 10)

12. Insert the basted Exterior Bag inside the Lining (with right sides together) and the wrong side of the Lining facing out. Match side seams and pin. (Figure 11) Sew a ½" seam around the entire Bag opening; stitch over this seam again to reinforce the seam. (Figure 11)

13. Turn the Bag right side out through the 8" opening in the Lining, then push the Lining inside the Bag and press. Pull out the Lining again and handstitch the opening closed, then reposition the Lining in the Bag.

DECORATIVE TIE

14. Following the Handle directions in step 5, fold and press the 8" x 20" Tie piece, then cut the ends at a 45-degree angle. (Figure 12)

15. Stitch a ½" seam along three sides, leaving a 2" opening on one side for turning. Trim the corners and seams, being careful not to clip the stitching.

16. Turn the Tie right side out, press, and handstitch the opening closed. Topstitch the Tie the same way you did on the Handle in step 5. ❤

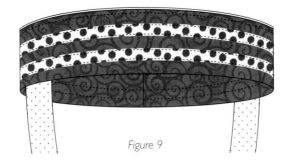

Figure 9

Figure 10

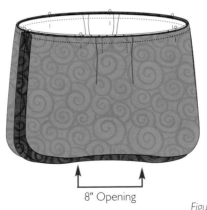

8" Opening

Figure 11

Pull fabric through opening

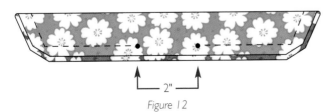

2"

Figure 12

41

Paneled Maxi Skirt

Showcase fun fabrics by making a strip skirt with a simple elastic waist. Choose different prints for different looks and add more panels for a fuller skirt if desired.

FINISHED DIMENSIONS

The skirt is 33" long; adjust as desired. The waist is elasticized and adjusts to any size.
Small: Fits up to 34" waist
Medium: Fits up to 39" waist
Large: Fits up to 42" waist

FABRIC

• ¾ to 1¼ yards each of three different coordinating fabrics (A, B, and C), depending on the desired skirt size and length (*Dotted Leaf* (A), *Voltage Dot* (B), and *Bleeding Heart* (C) from Westminster Fibers/Free Spirit *Chicopee Collection* by Denyse Schmidt were used in the sample)

Yardages are based on 45"-wide fabric; adjust as needed.

SUPPLIES

• General Sewing Supplies (page 138)
• ¾"-wide elastic (waist measurement minus 2")
• All-purpose thread in a matching color
• 2 safety pins (for threading elastic)
• Yardstick or ruler

CUTTING THE FABRIC

Mark cutting lines directly on the wrong side of the fabric, or make a paper pattern for the skirt panel and use that to cut the fabric. All skirt panels should be laid out and cut on the lengthwise grain of the fabric.

1. Cut two skirt panels from Fabric A (center front and center back panels), two panels from Fabric B (side front panels), and two panels from Fabric C (side back panels). If your fabric has a directional design, be sure to consider that as you mark and cut the panels.

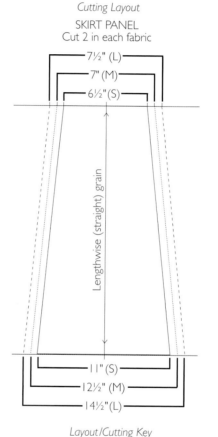

Cutting Layout
SKIRT PANEL
Cut 2 in each fabric

7½" (L)
7" (M)
6½" (S)

Lengthwise (straight) grain

11" (S)
12½" (M)
14½" (L)

Layout/Cutting Key
·············· = Small
- - - - - - = Medium
———— = Large

2. Straighten grainlines on all fabric pieces. With right sides together, fold the fabric in half lengthwise. At the top of the fabric (waistline), draw a straight line across the crosswise grain; make a mark in the center of this line.

ELLEN MARCH
Ellen is the editor in chief of *Sew News* (Jimmy Beans Wool's go-to website for sewing news), *Creative Machine Embroidery*, and *Sew It All* magazines; and the host of *Sew It All* on PBS stations nationwide. You can imagine our excitement when she gave us one of her original designs for *Sew Red*. At 34, this first-time mom spends a lot of time keeping up with her 10-month-old son. Though she is in excellent health and has no heart disease, she still sees the importance of raising awareness. An advocate for healthy eating and knowing where her food comes from, Ellen has been a vegetarian since she was 13. Ironically, her husband grew up on a cattle farm—proof that opposites attract! Thankfully, he loves fresh vegetables as much as she does and they both enjoy her homemade lasagna made with pureed vegetables and silken tofu.

 ELLEN'S TIP
Know where your food comes from and always eat fresh.

3. Measure down 36" (or your desired skirt length plus 3") and draw another straight line on the crosswise grain (for the hemline).

4. Draw a straight line along the lengthwise grain from the center of the waistline to the center of the hemline; mark the center on the hemline.

5. Mark the cutting lines for the waistline:
Small: Measure out 3¼" to each side of the center mark (6½" total length).
Medium: Measure out 3½" to each side of the center mark (7" total length).
Large: Measure out 3¾" to each side of the center mark (7½" total length).

6. Mark the cutting lines for the hemline (36" down from waistline for a 33"-long skirt, like the sample. If you're cutting a shorter or longer skirt, adjust the bottom measurements accordingly).
Small: Measure out 5½" to each side of the center mark (11" total length).
Medium: Measure out 6¼" to each side of the center mark (12½" total length).
Large: Measure out 7¼" to each side of the center mark (14½" total length).

7. Cut out two skirt panels from each fabric: A (center front and center back), B (side front panels), and C (side back panels) along the cutting lines marked in steps 1–5. Fabric A is for the center front and center back panels.

SEWING INSTRUCTIONS

All seams are sewn right sides together using a ½" seam allowance unless otherwise indicated. Backstitch at the beginning and end of each seam.

1. Zigzag-finish the long edges of each fabric panel; press.

2. Position the elastic around your waist so it's snug but not tight (about 2" shorter than your waist measurement). Cut the elastic and set aside.

3. With all raw edges aligned, pin then stitch one long edge of fabric A (center front) to one long edge of fabric B (side front). Stitch the opposite long edge of fabric A to one long edge of the other fabric B panel (side front). Press both seams flat and then press them open. This is the skirt front. (Figure 1)

4. To make the skirt back, follow the step 4 instructions except stitch fabric A to the two fabric C panels (side back). (Figure 2)

5. Pin then stitch the skirt front to the skirt back along the side seams, aligning all raw edges. Press the seams flat and then press them open.

6. To make the waistline casing for the elastic, fold the skirt upper edge ½" to the wrong side; press. Fold the upper edge another 1" to the wrong side; press. Stitch close to the second (lower) fold, leaving a 4" opening along the skirt center back panel for inserting the elastic; backstitch at each end of stitching. (Figure 3)

7. Fasten one safety pin to one end of the elastic; pin the other end of the elastic near the center back waistline. Feed the elastic completely through the casing, using the safety pin to push and pull; remove both pins. Make sure the elastic isn't twisted; overlap the ends of the elastic ½" and stitch through both layers (stitch a rectangle with an X through the center). (Figure 4) Push the elastic ends inside the casing; stitch the opening closed.

8. To hem the skirt, fold the skirt lower edge ¾" to the wrong side; press. Fold another 1" to the wrong side; press. Stitch close to the upper fold to hem the skirt. ♥

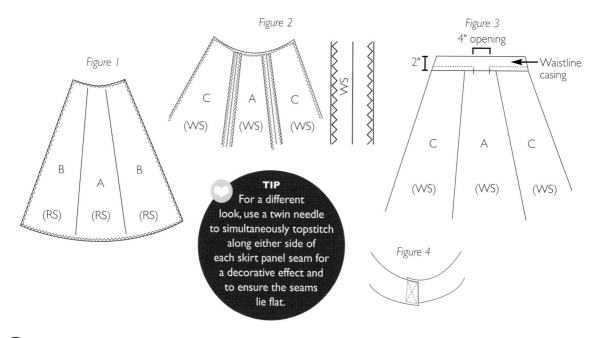

Figure 1

Figure 2

Figure 3
4" opening
2"
Waistline casing

TIP
For a different look, use a twin needle to simultaneously topstitch along either side of each skirt panel seam for a decorative effect and to ensure the seams lie flat.

Figure 4

Fleur Rouge Quilt

This traditional-looking quilt is made in reds, whites, and greens. Stars dot the center square, while a dainty floral zigzags over the border. It's perfect for any season!

FINISHED DIMENSIONS
46" square

FABRIC
All fabrics used in the sample are from *The Fleur Rouge Collection* by Anna Griffin.
- 1⅛ yards quilting cotton for Block Background (*Fleur Bleu* used in the sample)
- ¼ yard each of three coordinating quilting cottons for the Crowns (*Check Rouge, Ombré Rouge,* and *Rose Silo Rouge* used in the sample)
- ½ yard each of coordinating quilting cotton for the Block Stars (*Medallion Rouge, Paisley Rouge,* and *Bloom Rouge* used in the sample)
- ⅝ yard of coordinating quilting cotton for Inner Border and Binding (*Medallion Rouge* used in the sample)
- 1⅛ yards of coordinating cotton for Outer Border/LOF/WOF (*Espalier Rouge* used in the sample)
- 3 yards coordinating quilting cotton for Backing (*Solid Ivory* from the *Kona Collection* by Robert Kaufman used in the sample)

Yardages are based on 45"-wide fabric (42" usable fabric width); adjust as needed.

SUPPLIES
- General Sewing Supplies (page 138)
- Rotary cutter and cutting mat
- Ruler
- Stylus (optional)
- 48" × 48" square of batting
- Air-soluble fabric marking pen

CUTTING THE FABRIC
1. BACKGROUND
Cut two 1⅝" × width of fabric strips; sub-cut these strips into thirty-six 1⅝" squares.
Cut four 5¼" × width of fabric strips; sub-cut these strips into thirty-six 3¾" × 5¼" rectangles.
Cut two 3" × width of fabric strips; sub-cut these trips into eighteen 3" × 3" squares. Sub-cut these 18 squares once diagonally to form 36 half square triangles (HSTs).
Cut four 2⅝" × width of fabric strips; sub-cut these strips into seventy-two 1⅝" × 2⅝" rectangles.

2. STARS
Cut one 5¼" × width of fabric strip from each of these 3 fabrics. Sub-cut each of these 3 strips into three 5¼" squares for a total of 9 squares.
Cut three 3¾" × width of fabric strips from each of these 3 fabrics. Sub-cut each of these 3 strips into twenty-four 3¾" squares for a total of 72 squares.

3. CROWNS
Cut one 3" × width of fabric strip from each of the 3 fabrics. Sub-cut each of the 3 strips into six 3" squares (for a total of 18 squares). Sub-cut each of these 18 squares diagonally to create 36 half square triangles (HSTs), 12 HSTs in each fabric.
Cut three 1⅝" × width of fabric strips from each of the 3 fabrics, for a total of 9 strips. Sub-cut each of the 9 strips into forty-eight 1⅝" squares for a total of 432 squares.

4. INNER BORDER AND BINDING
Cut four 1½" × width of fabric strips for the Inner Border.
Cut five 2½" × width of fabric strips for the Binding.

PLACEMENT DIAGRAM

5. OUTER BORDER

The actual Outer Border equals the Length of Fabric (LOF) for right and left side borders and the Width of Fabric (WOF) for top and bottom borders.

For directional fabric (as in the sample): Cut two 6" × length of fabric strips for the right and left side Outer Borders. Cut four 6" × width of fabric strips

for the top and bottom Outer Border. Join 2 strips for the side Outer Borders and the 2 strips for the top and bottom Outer Borders with right sides together, matching the pattern as closely as possible.

OR for non-directional fabric: Cut eight 6" × width of fabric strips. Join two strips together, matching the pattern as closely as possible for each Border strip.

6. BACKING

Cut the 3-yard length of Backing fabric in half on the crosswise grain to make two 42" × 54" rectangles.

7. BINDING

Cut five 2" × width of fabric strips.

SEWING INSTRUCTIONS

All seams are sewn right sides together

using a ¼" seam allowance unless otherwise indicated. Backstitch at the beginning and end of each seam.

PIECING THE QUILT

1. Make the Star Point Units for the large center star in each Star Block. You will need the thirty-six 3¾" × 5¼" rectangles cut from the background fabrics (Cutting step 1) and the seventy-two 3¾" squares

cut from the star prints (Cutting step 2).

With right sides together, place one of the 3¾" squares on the right edge of the 3¾" × 5¼" background rectangle. Draw a diagonal line from the lower left corner to the upper right corner for the stitching line. Sew the two pieces together on the stitching line, and trim ¼" away from the stitching on the outer edge. Open the seam and press.

Repeat this step for the lefthand side of the Star Point Unit, except draw the stitching line from the upper left corner to the lower right corner. Repeat these steps until you have completed 80 Star Point Units for the 20 Blocks.

2. To create the four Crown Corners used in each Star Block, with right sides together, chain piece the 36 HSTs cut

from the background fabrics (Cutting step 1) with the 36 HSTs cut from the crown prints (Cutting step 3). Press the seams open and set the joined HSTs aside.

3. Make the 8 Crown Point Units for each of the 20 Blocks. You will need the seventy-two 1⅝" × 2⅝" rectangles cut from the background fabrics (Cutting step 1) and the one hundred forty-four 1⅝" squares cut from the crown prints (Cutting step 3). With right sides together, place one of the 1⅝" squares on the right edge of one 1⅝" × 2⅝" rectangle. Draw a stitching line from the lower left corner to the upper right corner; stitch together on the stitching line, trim the seam ¼" from the stitching and press the seam. Repeat on the left edge of the rectangle, except mark the diagonal stitching line from the upper left corner to the lower right corner. Complete sewing all 72 rectangles in the same manner.

4. Assemble the 36 Corner Squares needed for the 9 Star Blocks. Each Corner Square consists of 2 Crown Point Units (created in step 3), one 1⅝" background square (Cutting step 2) and one of the HST Units created in step 2. Join the Crown Point Unit to the right side of a HST Unit of the same fabric. Join a second Crown Point Unit of the same fabric to a 1⅝" background square on the right side; join this Unit to the top edge of the first Unit created in this step. Repeat these

steps to form two identical Corner Blocks. Create two of these Corner Blocks in reverse, starting on the left edge instead of the right. All four Corner Units just created will be needed for 1 larger Star Block.

5. The 9 Star Blocks are sewn in the following order and are made up of 3 Horizontal Sections (Rows), each containing 3 Units (or pieces). Join a Crown Point Corner Square (created in step 4) to the left edge of a Star Point Unit (created in step 1). The Crown Point Square should have the points facing toward the outside edge. Join another Crown Point Block to the right edge of this Unit, making sure that the points face toward the outer edge. Press away from the Corner Blocks. The middle horizontal section is made up of one 5¼" square cut from the star fabric (Cutting step 2); it should match the Star Point Unit you are currently working with from step 1. Stitch a matching Star Point Unit to each side of this 5¼" square, making sure the points face outward. Press the seams away from the center square. The final Horizontal Row is created in the same manner as the first Horizontal Row and should be joined along the bottom edge of the Middle Horizontal Row.

Once the entire block has been assembled, press the final seams open to ensure the block lies as flat as possible.

6. Arrange the 9 Star Blocks as desired. You will be joining four Blocks for each

Row and making a total of 5 Rows for the quilt. Alternate the seam pressing of each row to ensure the rows nest together. Press Row 1 to the left, Row 2 to the right, etc.

7. Stitch two of the 1½"-wide Inner Border strips (Cutting step 4) to the sides of the quilt; press. Stitch the remaining strips to the top and the bottom of the quilt; trim all ends even.

8. Stitch the 2½"-wide Outer Border (Cutting step 4) to the Inner Border in the same order and manner as the Inner Border, being careful not to stretch the bias edges of the LOF strips, to complete the Quilt Top.

9. With right sides together, stitch the five Binding strips together at their short ends, forming one long strip; press the strip in half lengthwise, with wrong sides together.

10. Stitch the two Backing pieces on their 54"-long edges, creating a Backing piece that is approximately 54" × 84"; press seam flat. Lay the Backing wrong side up and place the batting on top, with raw edges aligned. Center the Quilt Top, right side up, on top of the batting, and secure all layers together by basting or with safety pins.

11. Quilt as desired; trim all edges even. Apply the Binding (page 141) around the perimeter of the quilt. ❤

Parson Gray Ditty Bag

These insanely useful drawstring bags are great for travel, home, or even as gift bags. They're a cinch to make with leftover fabric, so just raid your scrap bag, and ta-da!

FINISHED DIMENSIONS
10½" × 11½"

FABRIC
For the Heart-Appliqué Bag:
- ⅓ yard of cotton fabric (C) for the Bag (David Butler's *Curious Nature Collection: PWPG002 Royal* used in sample)
- ¼ yard of cotton fabric (B) for the Appliqués (*Free Spirit Designer Essentials: Dapples—D14 Red* used in sample)

For the Red-Top Bag:
- ½ yard of cotton fabric (A) for the Bag Bottom (David Butler's *Curious Nature Collection: PWPG006 Steel* used in sample)
- ¼ yard of cotton fabric (B) for the Bag Top (Free Spirit *Designer Essentials: Dapples—D14 Red* used in sample)

Yardages are based on 45"-wide fabric; adjust as needed.

SUPPLIES
- General Sewing Supplies (page 138)
- Rotary cutter and cutting mat
- Matching all-purpose thread
- 1 yard of ⅛" cord
- 1 cord stop
- Safety pin

CUTTING THE FABRIC
For the Heart-Appliqué Bag:
1. Cut one 16"-high × 22"-wide rectangle from steel blue fabric (A).

2. Cut eight 1½" squares from red fabric (B).

For the Red-Top Bag:
1. Cut one 5½"-high × 22"-wide rectangle from red fabric (B).

2. Cut one 11½"-high × 22"-wide rectangle from royal blue fabric (C).

SEWING INSTRUCTIONS
All seams are sewn with right sides together using ½" seam allowances unless otherwise indicated. Backstitch at the beginning and end of each seam.

HEART-APPLIQUÉ BAG
1. Press under ¼" on upper edge of 16" × 22" rectangle. This is your main bag.

DAVID BUTLER

David started off as a high-profile graphic designer for big-name corporations like Warner Brothers, Cirque du Soleil, and *Rolling Stone* magazine. So how did he end up in the world of fabric and textiles? Married to Amy Butler (page 90), he's been behind the scenes of print and fabric design for many years. With David's family history of high blood pressure, stroke, and heart disease, it seems fitting that this noted, innovative husband-wife duo are part of *Sew Red*. David's history inspires him to work at keeping any symptoms at bay with diet and exercise. The key for him is mixing up routines to stay interested: from surfing to mountain biking, to running and weight training. He ignores "superhuman fad diets" that rarely ever work long-term and finds exercise that makes him happy. Leading a healthy lifestyle shouldn't be a job.

♥ DAVID'S TIP
At least every 90 minutes, get up off your butt and get away from your computer. A change of scenery and a midday workout will get the wheels turning to propel you through the rest of your day.

2. Center one ½" square appliqué piece on the right side of the main bag fabric, so the bottom point is 5¼" from the bottom raw edge. Needle-turn appliqué the square to the bag, turning the raw edges under a scant ¼". Continue to place the remaining squares on the main bag fabric (as shown in the photograph) to form a heart shape and needle-turn appliqué them to the bag.

3. With right sides together, pin then stitch the 15" edges together using a ½" seam allowance. This is the center back seam.

4. Measure down 2¼" from the upper (folded and pressed) edge, and clip the seam allowance horizontally from the raw edge to close to seam stitching line. Press the seam to one side.

5. Trim the bottom layer (only) of the seam allowance to ⅛". (Trim this bottom layer up to the point where you clipped the seam allowance in step 2.) Fold the untrimmed upper layer of the seam allowance around the bottom layer of the seam allowance, covering the raw edge of the bottom (⅛") seam allowance; press. Topstitch close to the pressed, folded edge. (This is a reverse flat-felled seam.)

6. To form the bottom of the bag (steps 6 and 7), turn the bag right side out. With wrong sides together and the back seam centered, pin then stitch the bottom of the bag using a ¼" seam allowance. Trim the seam to ⅛" and turn the bag inside out. With right sides now together, stitch a ¼" seam at the bottom of the bag, encasing the seam trimmed to ⅛" inside the ¼" seam. Press. This is a French seam.

7. Turn the bag right side out and lay it flat. Fold the bottom of the bag as shown in Figure 1. Mark down 1½" from each end of the bottom seam and mark a horizontal stitching line. Stitch across the stitching line through both layers of fabric. Trim seam to ⅛". Repeat at other end of bottom seam. (Figure 1)

8. Turn the bag inside out. Fold the seams stitched in step 7 with right sides together and stitch ¼" from the fold, encasing the trimmed seam inside. Press flat to complete the French seam.

9. With the bag remaining inside out, lay it flat so the back seam is facing up. At the top of the back seam where you left 2½" of the seam unstitched, fold under the raw edges of the seam allowance ½", then turn them under again, for a ¼" seam allowance; press. Edgestitch the seam allowance ⅛" from the folded edge.

10. Keep the bag inside out. To make the casing for the drawstring, fold over the upper pressed edge to the inside of the bag 1¼"; press. (Note that the top of the back seam creates an opening for the drawstring.) Edgestitch ⅛" from the bottom folded edge. Topstitch around the top of the bag, ½" from the upper edge to finish the casing.

11. Use a safety pin to pull the cording through the casing and, following manufacturer's instructions, attach the cord stop and knot the ends of the cord.

RED-TOP BAG
1. With wrong sides together, stitch the 22" edges of the red (B) and blue (C) fabric together using a ¼" seam. Trim the seam to ⅛". Fold the fabric along this seam so the right sides of the fabric are together and stitch a ¼" seam, enclosing the raw edges of the trimmed seam, forming a French seam. Press.

2. Follow steps 3–11 for the Heart-Appliqué Bag to finish the bag. ❤

Figure 1

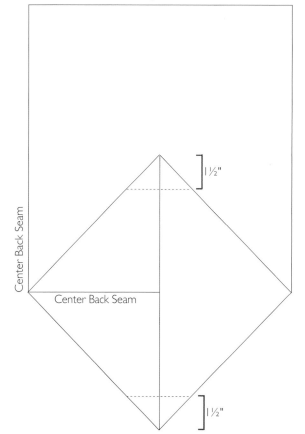

Center Back Seam

Center Back Seam

1½"

1½"

Heartfelt Rosy

A riot of color in florals, polka dots, and heart patterns, this quilt is bursting with life and energy. It's impossible not to smile when looking at it!

DESIGNED WITH LIZA PRIOR LUCY;
QUILTED BY JUDY IRISH

FINISHED DIMENSIONS
57" wide x 74½" long

FABRIC
All fabrics are from the Kaffe Fassett Collection
- 2 yards *Plink* in magenta
  (includes enough for the Binding)
- ½ yard each:
  Gone Fishing in red
  Cabbage and Rose in fuchsia
  Parasols in magenta
  Millefiore in tomato
  Asian Blooms in tomato
  August Rose in antique and magenta
  Brassica in red
  Cactus Dahlia in red
  Petunia in pink
- ¼ yard each:
  St Clements in red
  Sand Dollars in orange and red
  Millefiore in red
  Spots in green, orange, sapphire, purple, and periwinkle
  Paperweight in paprika
  Plink in red
  Baba Ganoush in magenta
  Picotee Poppies in red
- 4 yards *Disco Dots* in pink for quilt Backing

Yardages are based on 45"-wide fabric; adjust as needed.

SUPPLIES
- General Sewing Supplies (page 138)
- Rotary cutter and mat
- Quilting thread
- 4⅓ yards of batting

CUTTING THE FABRIC
This is a scrappy quilt. It isn't necessary to place each fabric as in the original.
Use the ½ yard fabrics for the Big Blocks and the Outer Border Squares. Use the ¼ yard fabrics for the 9-Patch Blocks.
Use the magenta *Plink* for the Inner Border.

1. BIG BLOCKS (9½" square): Cut 18.

2. OUTSIDE BORDER SQUARES (5" square): Cut 54.

KAFFE FASSETT
Perhaps best known in the world of fiber arts for his unique and unparalleled ability to manipulate texture and envision stunning colorways, it is no surprise that this guru of textiles and color has created such a beautiful quilt. Born in San Francisco, Kaffe won a scholarship from the School of the Museum of Fine Arts, Boston, but he did not stay for long. After three months, he moved to London to pursue painting. Inspired by the colors and landscapes of the English countryside, Kaffe not only learned to knit, but began creating spectacular floral fabric prints that would soon become household icons to patchwork sewers and quilters everywhere. Kaffe keeps himself busy with his various fiber crafts and makes sure to keep his diet healthy and simple. Salmon, salad, and a glass of heart-healthy wine keep this fiber artist in tip-top shape.

 **KAFFE'S TIP**
Cook with fresh, local produce as often as you can. Summer farmers' markets and roadside fruit and vegetable stands are great places to stock up on delicious, healthy food.

3. CORNERS: Fussy-cut 4 large flowers about 5" across.

4. 9-PATCH BLOCKS (make 18): Choose two fabrics and cut: Five 3½" squares from one fabric (cut 90 squares total for 18 blocks). Four 3½" squares from the other fabric (cut 72 squares total for 18 blocks).

5. SIDE INNER BORDERS: Cut two 3¼" × 63½" strips of turquoise *Plink*.

6. TOP AND BOTTOM INNER BORDER: Cut two 3¼" × 45½" strips of turquoise *Plink*.

7. BINDING: Cut seven 2¼" × width of fabric strips.

SEWING INSTRUCTIONS
All seams are sewn right sides together using a ¼" seam allowance unless otherwise indicated. Backstitch at the beginning and end of each seam.

ASSEMBLING THE TOP
1. Make each 9-Patch Block by arranging nine squares into three rows of three squares each, alternating colors. Sew each row together and then sew the three rows together. Make a total of 18 blocks in this way.

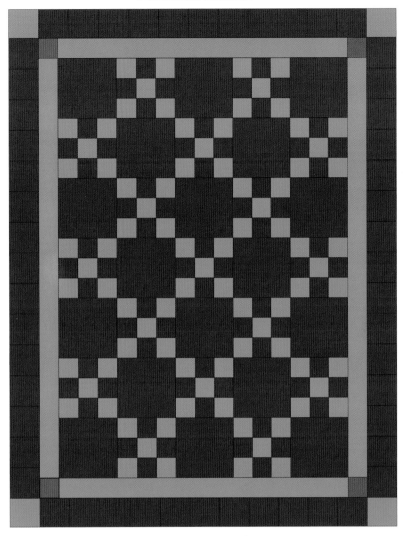

2. To assemble the rows, alternate the non-pieced Big Blocks with the 9-Patch Blocks. Following the arrangement in the picture, start with a Big Block in the upper left corner. Sew five blocks together for each row, then sew seven rows together.

3. Pin and stitch the Side Inner Borders to the center, then pin and stitch the Top and Bottom Inner Borders to the center. Sew the corner squares to the ends of the Side Inner Borders and the Top and Bottom Inner Borders.

4. Make the Outer Border by sewing 16 blocks together for each of the two sides. Sew 11 blocks together for the top and 11 for the bottom.

5. Pin and stitch the Side Borders to the center (which has the inner border already attached).

6. Sew the Fussy Cut Flower Squares to the ends of the Top and Bottom Borders and attach the Top and Bottom Borders to the center to complete the Quilt Top.

7. With right sides together, stitch the Binding strips together at their short ends, forming one long strip; press the strip in

half lengthwise, with wrong sides together. Trim to 275".

8. Lay the Backing wrong side up and place the batting on top, with raw edges aligned. Center the Quilt Front, right side up, on top of the batting, and secure all layers together by basting or with safety pins.

9. Quilt as desired. Trim all edges even. Apply the Binding (page 141) around the perimeter of the quilt. ❤

 **BRETT BARA**

Origami Pillow

You'd never think a little strategic folding could make such a complex design! This modern pillow uses origami magic for a sculptural effect that will enliven any space.

FINISHED DIMENSIONS
16" square

FABRICS
- Wool felt in two complementary shades of red
- Two 17" squares for the pillow Front and Back (1mm Wollfilz *Wool Felt* in Maroon from PurlSoho.com used in the sample)
- One 15" square for the Origami Appliqués (1mm Wollfilz *Wool Felt* in Cinnamon from PurlSoho.com used in the sample)

SUPPLIES
- General Sewing Supplies (page 138)
- All-purpose thread to match (Coats & Clark Dual Duty Plus used for sample)
- 16" pillow form
- 14" all-purpose zipper (optional)
- Quilter's ruler (or other straightedge measuring device)
- Air-soluble fabric marker or chalk marking pencil

CUTTING THE FABRIC
1. ORIGAMI APPLIQUÉS
Cut the Origami Appliqué square into five 3"-wide strips, then cut each strip into five 3" squares, for a total of twenty-five 3" squares.

SEWING INSTRUCTIONS
All seams are sewn right sides together using a ¼" seam allowance unless otherwise indicated. Backstitch at the beginning and end of each seam.

1. Place the ruler diagonally across the Front from corner to corner. Starting and ending 2" from each corner, draw a diagonal line across the fabric. (Don't draw the line all the way to the corners or it might be visible on your finished piece.) Place the ruler diagonally across the piece so it crosses the marked line; make a small mark at the center of the first line to mark the center of the fabric. (Figure 1)

2. Beginning at the center point, place and pin five 3" squares along the marked line. Stitch the squares to the Front, sewing from corner to corner through the centers of the squares. (Figure 2)

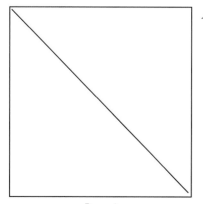

Figure 1

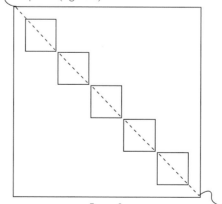

Figure 2

3. Working out from the first diagonal row of squares, continue to build diagonal rows of squares, being sure to align all squares to form a solid grid. Stitch each row in place along a diagonal line through the centers of the squares. (Figure 3) Use all 25 squares.

4. When all the squares are stitched in place, it's time to create the folded origami shape of each square. Starting at one corner of the Front and working toward the opposite corner, stitch across the squares diagonally from corner to corner, perpendicular to the stitching from steps 2 and 3, simultaneously folding the free tips (corners) of each square up (or down) toward its center as you sew, and sewing each folded corner in place as you go. (Figure 4 and detail)

5. Continue to stitch in diagonal rows of squares, parallel to the stitching from step 4, folding and stitching the corners in the same way.

NOTE: The pillow can be completed with or without a zipper. If you're not using a zipper, skip to step 10.

6. To insert the zipper, pin the Front and Back pieces together with right sides facing. On one side edge, begin sewing at the corner using a ½" seam allowance. Sew down the edge with a regular stitch for 1", then backstitch to secure, then switch to a basting stitch length. Continue to sew the seam with a basting stitch until you reach 1" from the next corner. Switch to a regular stitch length, backstitch to secure, then sew to the corner and fasten off.

7. Press the seam open, then center your zipper over the basted portion of the seam, pinning it in place so the zipper teeth are evenly centered over the seam. Starting at the upper end of the zipper, use a zipper foot to sew down one side of the zipper ¼" from basted seam, across the lower end, back up the other side, and across the zipper again to meet at the place where you began sewing, making a complete rectangle of stitching around the zipper.

8. Use a seam ripper to carefully remove the basting stitches and open the zipper.

9. Pin the pillow Front and Back together around the three remaining sides, with right sides facing; sew these edges. Trim corners. Turn the pillow right side out and press the seams flat. Insert the pillow form into the pillow cover.

10. For a pillow without a zipper, pin the pillow Front and Back together with right sides facing; stitch all four sides, leaving a 10" opening along one side. Trim corners. Turn the pillow right side out and press the seams flat. Insert the pillow form into the pillow cover and handstitch the opening closed. ♥

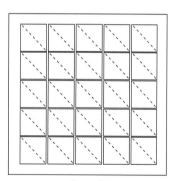

Figure 3

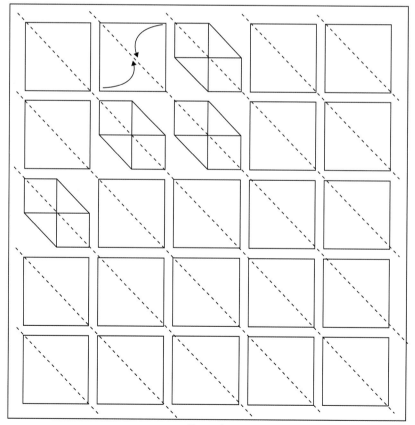

Figure 4

Kimono Sleeve Tunic

You'll feel like M. C. Escher in this tessellation tunic! Sailor-inspired with a lace accent, this top is fun to wear, easy to make, and flattering. A must-make!

SUEDEsays COLLECTION
FOR SIMPLICITY PATTERNS

FINISHED DIMENSIONS

X-Small: Fits bust 30½"–31½"
Small: Fits bust 32½"–34"
Medium: Fits bust 36"–38"
Large: Fits bust 40"–42"
X-Large: Fits bust 44"–46"
Finished garment measurements are printed on the pattern sheets included at the back of the book. Check them before cutting your fabric.

FABRIC

• 3⅛ yards of 44"-wide soft, lightweight fabric such as charmeuse, double georgette, laundered silks and rayons, batiks, or voile. (Charmeuse was used for the sample; you can use any of the lightweight fabrics listed for this design.)

SUPPLIES

• General Sewing Supplies (page 138)
• All-purpose thread to match fabric
• ¾ yard 20"-wide lightweight fusible interfacing
• 2 yards trim of your choice
• ⅞ yard of ⅜"-wide elastic
• 1⅝ yards of ¼" cord
• Safety pin

SUEDE

We first heard of Suede when he starred in season five of the Emmy Award–winning *Project Runway,* back when *Sew Red* wasn't on our radar. Now, Suede is a wildly popular fashion icon, the fashionista behind SUEDEsays™, and we are privileged to have an original design from him in *Sew Red.* This cause holds a special place in Suede's heart. When Suede was young, his father had a very serious heart attack and was airlifted to Texas for quadruple bypass surgery. Since then, making healthy choices has been engrained into his everyday routine. Suede makes sure to have a bowl of his favorite fruits in the house at all times, just in case he needs a quick snack. It is impossible to feel guilty about indulging in some delicious mango slices.

♥ SUEDE'S TIP

It is important to check the ingredients on packaged food labels before buying them. If you don't know what niacinamide is, chances are you don't need it in your pantry.

Front

Back

CUTTING DIAGRAM

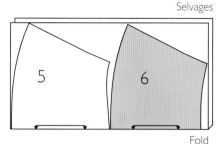

Selvages

5   6

Fold

Selvages

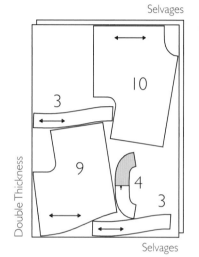

Double Thickness

10

3

9   4

3

Selvages

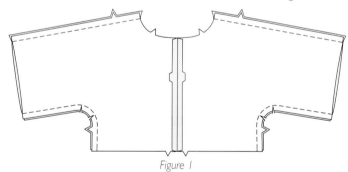

Figure 1

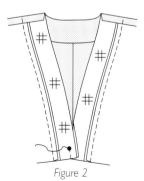

Figure 2

CUTTING THE FABRIC

1. Place the pattern pieces (see pattern sheets included with this book) on the fabric as shown in the Cutting Diagram and pin in place (or use weights). Cut out along the cutting lines for your size. Note that most of the pattern pieces are placed with the printed side of the tissue facing up; the shaded pieces should be placed with the printed side facing down.

Prepare your fabric by cutting it into two sections. First, fold fabric lengthwise with the right sides together and cut pieces 5 and 6 as shown. Then take the remaining full length of fabric and cut it in half on the crosswise grain, from selvage to selvage. Turn one section so the direction of any print or shading is going in the same direction on both pieces. Align all edges and place remaining pattern pieces as indicated on the Diagram.

2. Cut interfacing pieces from pattern pieces 3 and 4 as indicated on pieces.

3. Transfer all markings and notches to the fabric, including center lines and large or small dots, using the marking device(s) of your choice, or make small (¼") clips into seam allowance at markings.

SEWING INSTRUCTIONS

All seams are stitched right sides together with a ¾" seam allowance unless otherwise noted. Backstitch at the beginning and end of each seam.
Press all seams flat after stitching to set in the stitches, and then press seams open unless otherwise indicated.
Raw edges of seams can be finished with your serger or by stitching the seam again, ⅛" from first stitching, and trimming away fabric close to the second stitching.

1. To prevent the front edge of Front and Sleeve sections from stretching, machine-stitch ½" from the cut edge. Stitch the upper edge of Back and Sleeve sections in the same manner. Stitch the center back seam. Stitch each Front and Sleeve section to the Back and Sleeve. (Figure 1)

2. Apply fusible interfacing to the wrong side of two of the Front and one Back Band sections, following the manufacturer's directions. With right sides together, stitch the Front Band sections to the Back Band at the shoulder seams, matching notches. The remaining sections will be used as facings.

With right sides together pin the outer notched edge of the Band to the Front and Back, matching notches, centers, and shoulder seams. Clip the edge of the Front and Back at small intervals along the curves so that it can open up and conform to the shape of the neck band. Stitch the seam carefully along ⅝" seam line. Press the Band and the seam allowance out. Trim the seam to ⅜". Bring center front edges of the Band together, matching the large dot, and stitch the short seam from the lower edge of the Band to the large dot; backstitch at the dot and end to reinforce the seam. (Figure 2)

3. Stitch the shoulder seams of the Band Facing sections. To finish the outer notched edge of the Band, serge over the edge, trimming away ¼", or press under ¼" and stitch near fold.

4. Stitch the center front seam below the large dot just as you did for the Band. With right sides together, pin the Band Facing over the Band, matching shoulder seams, center front and back, and large dots. Start stitching at the large dot on one side of the Front and stitch the entire seam ending at the large dot on the other side. Backstitch at the dots to reinforce, careful not to catch the seam allowances underneath in the stitching. Carefully trim and clip the entire seam. (Figure 3)

5. Understitch (page 139) by pressing the seam toward the Band Facing, while

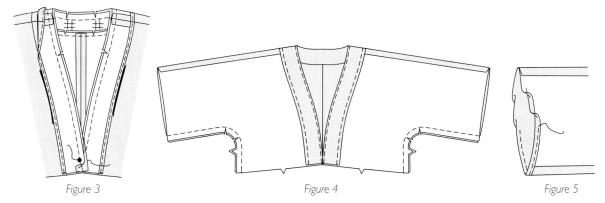

Figure 3

Figure 4

Figure 5

pressing the Facing out. On the Facing side, stitch close to the seam through all thicknesses. (This understitching keeps the facing from rolling to the outside.) Turn the Facing to the inside; press.

6. Carefully pin the edge of the Band over the seam, making sure it is flat and extending beyond the seam. Pin in place, placing the pins in the outside. You can baste in place if desired.

7. From the outside, stitch in the ditch (page 139) or groove of the entire band seam, catching in the facing, removing the pins as you come to them; press. With right sides together, stitch the entire underarm seam. To reinforce the curve at the underarm, stitch again over the first stitching. Make small clips into the seam at the curves. Press seam. (Figure 4)

8. Press the ⅝" hem allowance on the lower edge of the Sleeve to the inside, forming a crease. Open it out and turn the raw edge to the inside so that it just meets the crease, then turn the edge again to the inside along the crease. Stitch the hem in place close to the inner pressed edge. (Figure 5)

9. To reinforce the Buttonhole opening for the drawstring, fuse a small piece of interfacing to the wrong side of the Front over the Buttonhole marking. Make a Buttonhole at each marking. With right sides together, stitch the side seams of the Skirt sections. With right sides together, pin the Skirt sections to the Bodice,

matching centers and side seams. Stitch in a ¾" seam. (Figure 6)

10. To form the casing for the drawstring between the Bodice and the Skirt, trim the lower seam allowance to ¼". Press the Bodice seam allowance down, pressing under ¼" on the raw edge. Stitch close to the pressed edge. (Figure 7)

11. On the outside, stitch the trim in place with one edge along Band seam, turning under the raw edges at the waistline seam. Cut a piece of elastic the length of the guide on the pattern. Cut cord for the drawstring in half. Stitch a piece of cord to each end of the elastic. Attach a safety pin to one end of the cord, slip it through one buttonhole, and use it to help pass the cord through casing and out other buttonhole. (Figure 8)

12. Allow the garment to hang overnight to allow the hem to stretch along curves. Mark the length, allowing for a ⅝" narrow hem. Trim the hem as needed. To form a narrow hem, press up ⅝" at the bottom of the Skirt, forming a crease. Open out and press under the raw edge to meet the crease. Press under the edge again along the crease. Stitch in place close to inner pressed edge. (Figure 9) ❤

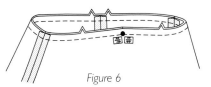

Figure 6

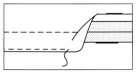

Figure 7

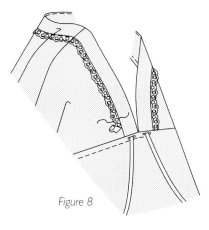

Figure 8

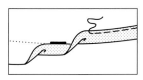

Figure 9

♥ **JENEAN MORRISON**

Buttoned-Up

These mix and match place mats and napkins feature a buttoned tab to hold the napkin and flatware in place. They're perfect to take to a picnic or use every day!

FINISHED DIMENSIONS
20½" × 14"

FABRICS
- 1⅞ yards mid-weight printed cotton (*Pink Grand Hotel* by Jenean Morrison used in the sample)
- 1⅞ yards contrasting mid-weight printed cotton (*Sunset Grand Hotel* by Jenean Morrison used in the sample)

Yardages are based on 45"-wide fabric; adjust as needed.

SUPPLIES
- General Sewing Supplies (page 138)
- ⅞ yard of 45"-wide fusible fleece (Pellon 973F used in the sample)
- 6¾" × 12" rectangle of fusible mid-weight interfacing (Pellon 931TD used in the sample)
- All-purpose thread (Coats & Clark Dual Duty XP, color 2250 Red used in the sample)
- ⅞" cover button kit with 4 buttons (Dritz 14-36 used in the sample)
- Rotary cutter and cutting mat
- Ruler

CUTTING THE FABRIC
1. From each of the two fabrics:
Cut two 14½" × 21" rectangles (A) for the Place Mat Backs (total of 4).
Cut two 14½" squares (B) for the Front Plate Panels (total of 4).
Cut two 14½" × 7" rectangles (C) for the Front Napkin Panels (total of 4).
Cut four 3" × 6¾" rectangles (D) for the Button Tabs (total of 8).
Cut four 18" squares (E) for the Napkins (total of 8).

2. Fusible fleece:
Cut four 14½" × 21" rectangles for the Place Mats.

3. Interfacing:
Cut four 3" × 6¾" rectangles for the Button Tabs.

JENEAN MORRISON
Jenean is a multifaceted artist who designs stationery, fabrics, rugs, and gift wrap; designing for Free Spirit is just part of her artistic career. She is proud to be from Memphis and has showcased her *Grand Central* collection (which we hope to get) along with other local Memphis artists in the windows of vacant downtown buildings. Her soft, retro-colored designs are eye-catching (and sometimes play games with our eyes). With such unique designs it's no surprise Jenean selected these multifunctional place mats for *Sew Red*. Jenean's father struggles with heart disease, and that has inspired her to change her habits so she can live a long, healthy life. While it's easy for Jenean to pass the hours working on a project, she makes an effort to get herself up and moving throughout the day; she and her husband walk together twice a day, seven days a week.

♥ **JENEAN'S TIP**
Set a timer so you don't stay seated too long. When it goes off, get up and dance around. (This might be easier for those who work from home...)

SEWING INSTRUCTIONS

All seams are sewn right sides together with a ¼" seam allowance unless otherwise noted. Backstitch at beginning and end of each seam.

PREPARING THE BUTTON TABS

1. The Button Tabs (D) on each place mat are made from two 3" x 6 ¾" rectangles (D) of matching fabric. Pair up the 8 Button Tab fabric rectangles to make two Button Tabs from each fabric. Turn one rectangle from each pair wrong side up and place the adhesive side of one interfacing rectangle on the wrong side of the fabric. Following the manufacturer's instructions, fuse the interfacing to the fabric.

2. For each tab, place an interfaced rectangle and uninterfaced rectangle (of matching fabric) right sides together and stitch around three sides, leaving one short end open. Trim the excess fabric from the corners and turn the Tab right side out; press. Topstitch ¼" from the finished edges.

3. Mark a 1" line in the center of each tab, ½" from the finished end, and stitch a 1" buttonhole on the marking.

MAKING THE PLACE MATS

4. Place the 14½" edge of a Front Napkin Panel (C) along the 14½" edge of a fleece rectangle. The wrong side of the fabric should be against the adhesive side of the fleece.

Following the manufacturer's instructions, fuse the fabric to the fleece, taking care that the hot iron does not touch the adhesive of the uncovered side of the fleece. (Figure 1)

5. Pin a Button Tab in the same fabric print onto the Front Napkin Panel, aligning the unfinished edge of the tab with the cut edge of the contrast rectangle. Place the tab 3¼" from the lower edge of the Front Napkin Panel. (Figure 1) Baste in place.

6. With the fabrics right sides together, pin a 14½" edge of a Front Plate Panel (B) in the opposite fabric to the inside raw edge of the fleece-fused Front Napkin Panel. Stitch together.

7. Fold back the Front Plate Panel right side out over the fleece and press the seam flat. Continue to press the Front Plate Panel, fusing it to the fleece. Topstitch ¼" away from the seam on each side of the seam. This is the Place Mat Front.

8. With right sides together, pin a Place Mat Back to the Place Mat Front. Stitch, leaving a 3" opening on one side for turning. Trim the corners and turn the mat right side out. Slipstitch the opening closed. Topstitch ¼" from all edges of the mat.

9. Following the manufacturer's instructions, cover the buttons with scraps of leftover fabric. Make two buttons from each of the two fabrics.

10. Sew a button to each mat. The print of the button should match the Front Plate Panel of the Mat. Position the button 1" from the side edge and 4¼" from the bottom edge.

MAKING THE NAPKINS

1. For each napkin, pin two contrasting Napkin squares right sides together. Stitch all edges, leaving a 2" opening for turning.

2. Trim the corners and turn the Napkin right side out. Press, turning in the raw edges at the opening. Topstitch close to all edges of the Napkin. ❤

Figure 1

Paper Hearts

This vibrant Valentine's Day quilt elicits memories of elementary school paper hearts, valentines, and gorging yourself on candy conversation hearts. Do your loved ones some good, and sew this instead!

QUILTED BY ANGELA WALTERS

FINISHED DIMENSIONS
Approximately 48" x 63"

FABRIC
- 1 yard quilting cotton in gray (*S-11 Gray* from Free Spirit used in the sample)
- 1¼ yards quilting cotton in white (*H09 Caribbean* from Free Spirit used in the sample)
- ⅜ yard each of 8 different cotton prints (*TP09 Coral, TP13 Aqua, TP11 Coral, TP14 Coral, TP12 Aqua, TP10 Coral,* and *TP15 Coral,* all designed by Tula Pink for Free Spirit; and *GP70 Tomato* by Kaffe Fassett for Free Spirit used in the sample)
- 3½ yards quilting cotton for Backing (*GP70 Tomato* by Kaffe Fassett used in the sample)
- ½ yard coordinating cotton for Binding (*GP70 Tomato* by Kaffe Fassett)

Yardages are based on 45"-wide fabric; adjust as needed.

SUPPLIES
- General Sewing Supplies (page 138)
- All-purpose thread in coordinating colors
- 50" x 64" piece of batting
- Safety pins

CUTTING THE FABRIC
1. GRAY FABRIC
Cut 4 strips 5½" x width of fabric (A).
Cut sixty-four 2½" squares (B).

2. WHITE FABRIC
Cut thirty-two 6½" squares (C).

3. EACH PRINT
Cut four 6½" x 12½" rectangles (D), for a total of 32 rectangles.

4. BINDING
Cut 6 strips, each 2½" x width of fabric.

TULA PINK
Tula is at the forefront of design innovation in the fabric world, and we are honored to have one of her out-of-this-world designs in *Sew Red*. She hopes to inspire you (and herself!) to implement heart-healthy habits in your daily routine. Tula is fortunate to live in Stewartsville, Missouri, surrounded by family farms, where it's easy to eat fresh, locally raised foods every day. Her neighbors all have something to offer in the way of produce, and everyone loves to share. Tula's yard, for example, is home to several large apple trees, which her neighbors regularly visit to harvest fruit. Tula will often come home to a box of sweet corn, onions, or eggs in exchange for her apples. Usually standing up while she sews, Tula gets a surprisingly good workout constantly moving around her studio as she cuts, presses, sews, and lays out projects.

♥ TULA'S TIP
Keeping stress levels in check and having a daily dose of happy can do a world of good for the body and the soul.

PLACEMENT DIAGRAM

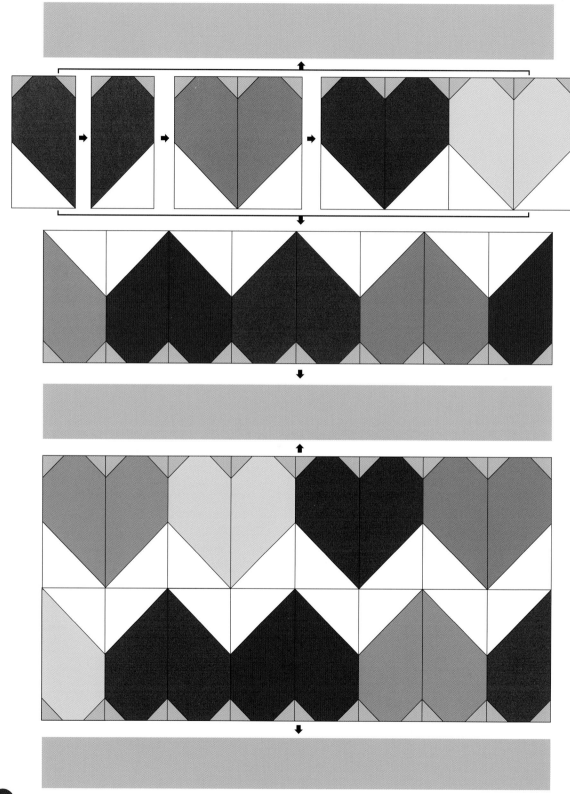

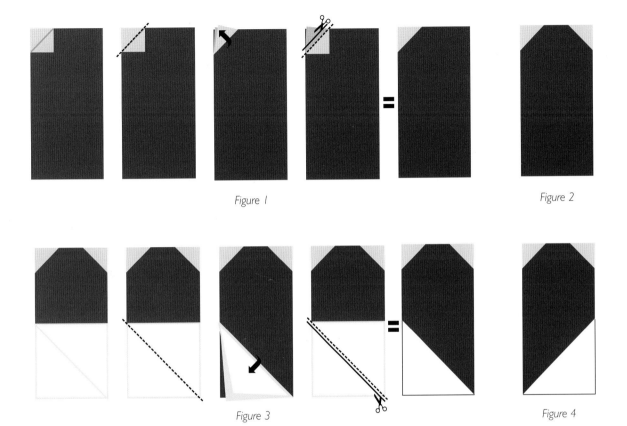

Figure 1

Figure 2

Figure 3

Figure 4

SEWING INSTRUCTIONS

All seams are sewn right sides together using a ¼" seam allowance unless otherwise indicated.

1. Stitch the 4 gray fabric strips (A) together at their short ends, forming a strip that is 5½" × 4 times the width of fabric. Trim this long strip to make 3 strips that measure 5½" × 48½".

2. On the gray squares (B) and the white squares (C), draw a diagonal line on the wrong side of each square from one corner to the opposite corner.

3. Place a 2½" gray square on the upper left corner of a print rectangle (D) and stitch them together on the diagonal line. (Figure 1)

4. Fold the inside corner back, lining up the outside corners; press. Trim both layers of the seam allowance even. (Figure 1)

5. Repeat steps 3 and 4 on the upper right corner of the print rectangle. (Figure 2) Follow steps 3 to 5 to complete 32 pieces.

6. Following steps 3 and 4, stitch a white 6½" square to each bottom left corner of the 16 print rectangles. (Figure 3)

7. Following steps 3 and 4, stitch a white 6½" square to the bottom right corner of the 16 print rectangles. (Figure 4)

8. Follow the assembly diagram to complete your Quilt Top.

9. With right sides together, stitch the six Binding strips together at their short ends, forming one long strip; press the strip in half lengthwise, with wrong sides together.

10. Lay the Backing wrong side up and place the batting on top, with raw edges aligned. Center the Quilt Top, right side up, on top of the batting, and secure all layers together by basting or with safety pins.

11. Quilt as desired; trim all edges even. Apply the Binding (page 141) around the perimeter of the wall hanging. ❤

Quilt details

Westminster Backpack

Whether you're hiking or toting books, this roomy backpack will do the job. Sturdy and easy to make, it features expandable side pockets that close with Velcro® and adjustable straps.

TY PENNINGTON
Many of us at Jimmy Beans Wool know Ty from his days on the hit shows *Trading Spaces* and *Extreme Makeover: Home Edition*, on which he provided home improvements for those in need. Today, we know him as a fabric designer, with his newest collection, Impressions, inspired by the resilience he witnessed in our nation's small towns, big cities, and rural communities when filming his shows. When this book project started, many of our staff members were adamant that we get a design from him. Luck was on our side because sure enough, Ty signed up. He's known for being generous with his time and for raising awareness for good causes, so you might not be surprised that Ty jumped on board, but we were. And honored, too. While Ty may not have a personal tie to heart disease, he understands the importance of taking care of his health. A daily morning workout followed by stretching keeps his ticker healthy.

❤️ **TY'S TIP**
You are the only you, so take care of yourself!

FINISHED DIMENSIONS
12" wide × 17" tall × 5½" deep

FABRIC
- ½ yard cotton print fabric (A) for the Outside Body (*Impressions #PWTY 025 Hot Rose* by Ty Pennington for Westminster Fibers used in the sample)
- ½ yard of coordinating cotton print fabric (B) for the Outside Bottom Border, Bag Bottom, and Straps (*Impressions #PWTY 026 Black* by Ty Pennington for Westminster Fibers used for sample)
- ½ yard of coordinating cotton print fabric (C) for the Flap and Side Pockets (*Impressions #PWTY 026 Flami* by Ty Pennington for Westminster Fibers used for sample)
- 1 yard of coordinating cotton print fabric (D) for the Bag Interior/Lining and Flap (*Impressions #PWTY 023 Hot Rose* by Ty Pennington for Westminster Fibers used for sample)

Yardages are based on 44"-wide fabric; adjust as needed.

SUPPLIES
- General Sewing Supplies (page 138)
- 1 yard 44"-wide fusible heavyweight interfacing (Pellon Décor Bond used for sample)
- 1½ yards of 1"-wide nylon strapping
- Two 1"-wide clasps (Dritz used for sample)
- Four 1"-wide rectangular rings (Dritz used for sample)
- One package ½"-wide fusible web tape (Warm Company Steam a Seam 2 used for sample)
- One package self-adhesive double-sided basting tape (Dritz Wonder Tape used for sample)
- 5" strip of hook-and-loop tape (Velcro® used for sample)
- ½ yard of ¼"-wide black grosgrain ribbon
- Permanent fabric adhesive (Beacon Fabri-Tac used for sample)
- Matching all-purpose sewing thread (Coats & Clark Dual Duty Plus used for sample)

CUTTING THE FABRIC
1. FABRIC A (OUTSIDE BODY)
Cut two 13"-long (lengthwise grain) × 14"-wide (crosswise grain) rectangles for the Front and Back.
Cut two 6½"-long × 14"-wide rectangles for the Sides.

2. FABRIC B (OUTSIDE BOTTOM BORDER, BAG BOTTOM, AND STRAPS)
Cut two 13"-long × 5"-wide rectangles for the Front and Back Borders.
Cut two 6½"-long × 5"-wide rectangles for the Side Borders.
Cut one 13"-long × 6½"-wide rectangle for the Bottom.
Cut two 4"-wide × 36"-long strips for the Straps.

3. FABRIC C (SIDE POCKETS AND FLAP)
Cut four 8"-wide × 10½"-long rectangles for the Pockets.
Cut one 13"-long × 11"-wide rectangle for the Flap.

4. FABRIC D (BAG INTERIOR AND FLAP)
Cut two 13" × 18" rectangles for the Front and Back.
Cut two 6½" × 18" rectangles for the Sides.
Cut one 6½" × 13" rectangle for the Bottom.

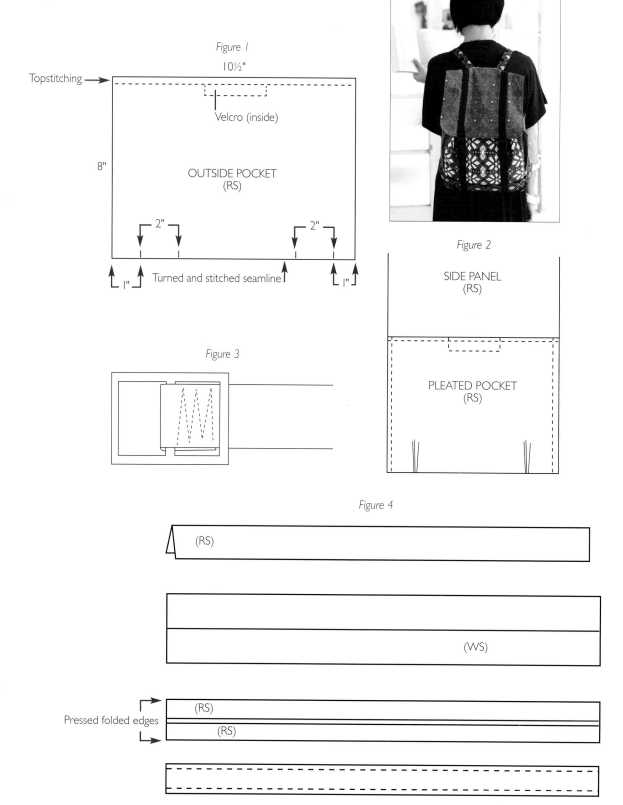

Figure 1

10½"

Topstitching →

Velcro (inside)

8"

OUTSIDE POCKET
(RS)

2"

2"

1"

Turned and stitched seamline

1"

Figure 2

SIDE PANEL
(RS)

PLEATED POCKET
(RS)

Figure 3

Figure 4

(RS)

(RS)

(WS)

Pressed folded edges

(RS)

(RS)

5. FUSIBLE INTERFACING

Cut two 13" × 18" rectangles
for the Front and Back.
Cut two 6½" × 18" rectangles for
the Sides.
Cut one 6½" × 13" rectangle
for the Bottom.
Cut one 13" × 11" rectangle for the Flap.
Cut two 4" × 36" strips for the Straps.

SEWING INSTRUCTIONS

Sew all seams with right sides together
using a ½" seam allowance unless
otherwise indicated. Backstitch at the
beginning and end of each seam.

1. Sew the Front and Back pieces (fabric
A) to the corresponding Border strips
(fabric B) on the bottom (14") edges, and
the two Side pieces (fabric A) to the
corresponding Border strips (fabric B) on
the bottom (6½") edges; press the seams
toward the borders.

2. Follow the manufacturer's instructions
to fuse the interfacing to the wrong side
of the corresponding pieces for the
Outside Body, Flap, and Straps.

3. To make each Pocket (fabric C), sew
the long (10½") edges together. Turn right
side out and press. Topstitch along one
long edge; this will be the top of the
Pocket. Cut the Velcro strip in half and
sew one loop side to the center of the
topstitched edge of each Pocket, just
below the stitching. (Velcro is applied to
the inside of each Pocket.)

4. To attach each Pocket to a Side Panel,
pin it in place 1" above the bottom of the
Side Panel with the raw side edges of the
Pockets and Side Panels aligned and the
topstitched edge of Pocket at the top.
Make two pleats, each 1" from the side
edge, on the bottom of the Pocket so it
fits the panel smoothly. (Figure 1 and
detail) Topstitch the bottom edge and
pleats in place; baste the side edges of the
Pockets and Side Panels in place. Press the
pleats in place all the way to the top of
the Pocket. Sew the hook side of the
Velcro to the Side Panels to align with the

loop strips on the Pockets. (Figure 2)

5. Cut two 12" lengths of nylon strapping
for the clasp closures. Thread one strip
around the bar on the bottom section of
a clasp, overlapping the strip on itself for
about 1". Stitch back and forth across the
overlapped strips to secure in place. On
the back of each nylon strap, apply a strip
of basting tape along the center. Remove
the paper backing from the basting tape
and adhere the Straps (vertically) to the
Front Panel 3" in from each side edge,
with the raw strap ends even with the
bottom of the Front Panel. Stitch the
straps in place along all edges. (Figure 3)

6. To make the pack's fabric Straps (fabric
B), press under one short (4") edge of
each strip ½" and fuse in place with fusible
web tape. Fold each strip in half
lengthwise with wrong sides together;
press. Open the strip and then fold the
long raw edges (wrong sides together) to
meet in the pressed fold at the center;
press. Fold the strip in half again along the
center lengthwise (pressed) fold so raw
edges are inside the folded strip; press.
Apply a strip of fusible web tape to the
inside of one long, folded edge of the strip
and press to fuse the folded edges
together. Topstitch close to all edges.
(Figure 4 and 3 details)

7. To attach the fabric Straps to the Back
Panel, cut a 4" length from the unhemmed
end of each Strap. Wrap the center of
each 4" Strap length around two
rectangular rings and stitch the Strap ends
together close to the rings. Baste the ends
of the Straps to the bottom edge on the
right side of the Back Panel fabric, 1" in
from the side edges, with raw edges
aligned at the bottom. Baste the raw ends
of the long Straps to the top of the Back
Panel (on the right side of the fabric), 4"
from the side edges. (Figure 5)

8. For the Flap (fabric D), trim the two
bottom edges into a curve (use a drinking
glass as a template; trace the outline and
cut along the tracing). Cut two 15" lengths
of nylon strapping. Apply a strip of basting

tape to the center of each strapping
length from the top of one end to 6" up
from the opposite end. Remove the
paper backing from the tape and adhere
the straps to the right side of the Flap 3"
from each side edge; the end without
the basting tape should be toward
the bottom of the Flap. Edgestitch each
strapping length in place; stop your
stitching 6" from the bottom edge, leaving
the bottom 6" of the nylon straps free.
(Figure 6)

9. To sew the outer bag together, sew
the Side Panels to the Front Panel, ending
the stitching ½" from the bottom edges.
Sew the Side Panels to the Back Panel,
starting and ending the stitching ½" from
the top and bottom edges. (Leaving ½"
unstitched at the ends makes it easier to
stitch the Bottom Panel to the assembled
Front, Back, and Side Panels.) (Figure 7)

10. Sew the Bottom Panel to the bottom
of the bag (Figure 8) and the Flap to the
top edge of the Back Panel. (Figure 9) Turn
right side out and press all seams.

11. To make the Lining, trim the
bottom corners of the Flap Panel to
match the outside Flap (step 8).
Follow Steps 8 to 10 to sew the Lining
pieces together, leaving a 6" opening in
the center of one bottom seam.
Do not turn the Lining right side out.

12. With right sides together, place the
Outer Bag inside the Lining, matching all
corresponding seams and edges; pin in
place around the top of the bag and the
Flap. (The Outer Bag is right side out
inside the lining.) Sew the top bag edges
and the flap edges together. Trim the
curves on the flap seam allowance.

13. Turn the backpack right side out
through the opening in the Lining seam
(step 11). Press the open seam allowances
under and hand or machine stitch the
opening closed. Place the Lining back
inside in the backpack and press the
seams. Topstitch along the top edges of
the backpack and around the flap edges. ❤

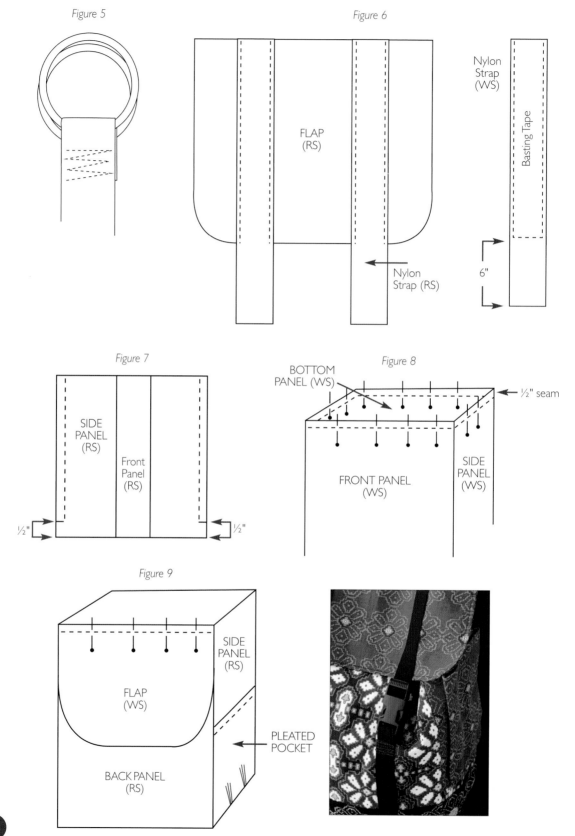

Figure 5

Figure 6

FLAP
(RS)

Nylon
Strap (RS)

Nylon
Strap
(WS)

Basting Tape

6"

Figure 7

SIDE
PANEL
(RS)

Front
Panel
(RS)

½"

½"

Figure 8

BOTTOM
PANEL (WS)

½" seam

FRONT PANEL
(WS)

SIDE
PANEL
(WS)

Figure 9

SIDE
PANEL
(RS)

FLAP
(WS)

PLEATED
POCKET

BACK PANEL
(RS)

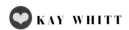
KAY WHITT

Sweet Sixteen Skirt

The Sweet Sixteen Skirt swings at the hemline for a flirty '50s finish. Composed of 16 panels and based on simple construction, it's easy to sew with fabulous results!

FINISHED DIMENSIONS
Small: 34" to 36" hips × 24" long
Other sizes to fit: 38" to 50" hips × 30" or 36" long, as indicated in instructions

FABRIC
All the fabrics used in this skirt are from the *Marmalade Collection* by Bonnie and Camille for Moda.

- **Cotton fabric (A)**
  for the Main Skirt and Waistband
  (*Raspberry 55050 12* used in the sample)

Skirt Size	24" length	30" length	36" length
34" – 36" Hips	2⅛ yards	2⅝ yards	3⅛ yards
38" – 50" Hips	2¼ yards	2⅔ yards	3¼ yards

- **Fabrics B and C**
  Two complementary or contrasting cotton fabrics (B and C) for the Godets for all sizes (Long Godets B: *Raspberry 55056 12* and Short Godets C: *Raspberry 55052 12* used in the sample)

Skirt	24" length	30" length	36" length
Tall Godets Fabric B	1 yard	1¼ yards	1⅝ yards
Short Godets Fabric C	⅝ yard	1 yard	1¼ yards

- **Fabric D** (Hem Band)
  ½ yard complementary or contrasting cotton fabric (*Raspberry 55054 12* used in the sample)

Yardages are based on 45"-wide fabric; adjust as needed.

SUPPLIES
- General Sewing Supplies (page 138)
- ¼" elastic

34" hips	3 yards
36" – 40" hips	3½ yards
42" – 46" hips	4 yards
48" – 50" hips	4½ yards

- Ruler or yardstick
- Rotary cutter and cutting mat (optional)
- Matching all-purpose thread
- Safety pin or bodkin

**TIP
Taking Measurements**
Measure around the fullest part of your hips. If your measurement falls between two numbers, round up to the nearest even number.

KAY WHITT
We have to be honest: This classic-yet-modern designer was on our radar from the moment we got the thumbs-up to gather designers for this book. We like to think it was serendipitous that Laura met Kay, of Serendipity Studios (formerly known as Serendipity Gifts), and was able to sign her up. Perhaps it was her personal connection to cardiovascular disease (or Laura's charm) that struck a chord. *Sew Red* was a great way for Kay to spread awareness of this silent killer that runs on both sides of her family. Her father underwent heart bypass surgery, and that had a huge impact on her lifestyle choices. With a summer pepper garden and regular usage of extra virgin olive oil in her cooking, Kay and her family have made the decision to be very conscious of what goes into their bodies.

KAY'S TIP
Staying active is a huge part of staying heart healthy!

CHART I

Hip Measurement	Skirt Panel Width Cut width (Crosswise grain)	24"-long Skirt Cut length (Lengthwise grain)	30"-long Skirt Cut length (Lengthwise grain)	36"-long Skirt Cut length (Lengthwise grain)
34"	5⅜"	23"	29"	35"
36"	5½"	23"	29"	35"
38"	5⅝"	23"	29"	35"
40"	5¾"	23"	29"	35"
42"	5⅞"	23"	29"	35"
44"	6"	23"	29"	35"
46"	6⅛"	23"	29"	35"
48"	6¼"	23"	29"	35"
50"	6⅜"	23"	29"	35"

CUTTING THE FABRIC

A rotary cutter is suggested for cutting all Skirt Panels and Godets, but scissors can be used.

CUTTING THE SKIRT PANELS (CUT 16)

1. Follow Chart 1 above to cut 16 rectangles that will form the Skirt Panels.

2. After all 16 Panels have been cut, stack them right side up in groups/piles of 4 with all raw edges even, making sure that the fabric design for all is going in the same direction. On the top Panel of each stack, mark in 1" from each side raw edge along the upper narrow edge. (Figure 1)

3. Use a ruler to align the 1" mark with the bottom corner of the fabric stack and trim away the small triangle. Repeat for the other side to form a long, skinny trapezoid. (Figure 2) Repeat for the remaining 3 stacks.

4. CUTTING THE GODETS (CUT 8 LONG GODETS AND 8 SHORT GODETS)

Follow Chart 2 to cut 8 rectangles in each size that will form a total of 16 Godets.

NOTE: Please refer to the width that you cut for your Skirt Panels (see Chart 1) to determine the width needed for each

CHART 2

Short Godets (cut 8 in Fabric C); Long Godets (cut 8 in Fabric B)

Skirt Length	Short Godets (Fabric C) (Length of rectangle; cut on lengthwise grain)	Long Godets (Fabric B) (Length of rectangle; cut on lengthwise grain)	Width of Rectangle for all Godets (See widths in Chart 1; cut on crosswise grain)
24"	10"	16"	See Chart 1
30"	16"	22"	See Chart 1
36"	22"	28"	See Chart 1

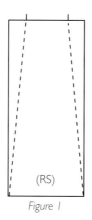

Figure 1

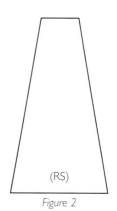

Figure 2

Figure 3

Godet. (For example, the 24"-length skirt in hip size 34 would have Godets measuring 10" x 5⅜" and 16" x 5⅜".)

5. After all the rectangles have been cut, stack the Short Godet rectangles right side up in two groups of 4 with all edges even, making sure that the fabric design

for all is going in the same direction. Repeat for the Long Godet rectangles. On the top Panels of each stack, mark the center of the top narrow edge, then mark ½" to either side of that center mark. (Figure 3)

6. Use a ruler to align the off-center mark with the bottom corner of the fabric and trim away the small triangle. Repeat for the other side to form a long, skinny trapezoid. (Figure 4)

7. After the Godets have been cut, turn them over so that the wrong sides are facing up. At the center of the top raw edge, mark ½" down from the edge on each of the 16 Godets. (Figure 5)

SEWING INSTRUCTIONS

All seams are sewn right sides together using a ½" seam allowance unless otherwise indicated. Backstitch at the beginning and end of each seam.

SEWING THE PANELS
AND GODETS TOGETHER

1. Place one Skirt Panel and one Godet (Short or Long) right sides together along the lower edge with the long side edges aligned. With the Godet side facing up, stitch the Godet and Skirt Panel together starting from the lower edge; stop when the stitching reaches the dot marking on the Godet. Backstitch at the beginning and end of the seam. (Figure 6)

2. Open the Godet out away from the Skirt Panel, and with right sides together, add another Skirt Panel to the remaining long side of the Godet with side and bottom edges even. Stitch the same way as in step 1, stopping at the marking. (Figure 7)

3. Align the remainder of the Skirt Panel seam (above the Godet) right sides together. Stitch from the top edge of the Panels downward until the junction of seams is reached. (Figure 8)

4. From the wrong side, open the Skirt Panel seam above the Godet and trim the seam to ¼" down the entire length. Serge or overcast each trimmed seam edge, continuing down the length of the skirt all the way to the lower edge. Press the seam open above the Godet, then press the seams of the Godet toward the Skirt Panels. (Figure 9)

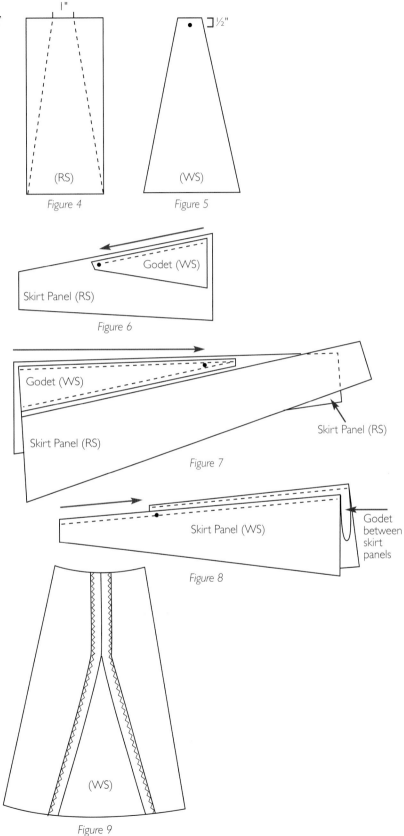

Figure 4

(RS)

1"

Figure 5

(WS)

1½"

Figure 6

Godet (WS)

Skirt Panel (RS)

Figure 7

Godet (WS)

Skirt Panel (RS)

Skirt Panel (RS)

Figure 8

Skirt Panel (WS)

Godet between skirt panels

Figure 9

(WS)

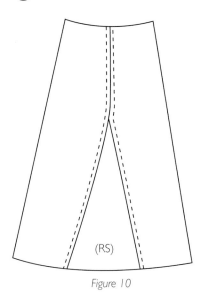

(RS)

Figure 10

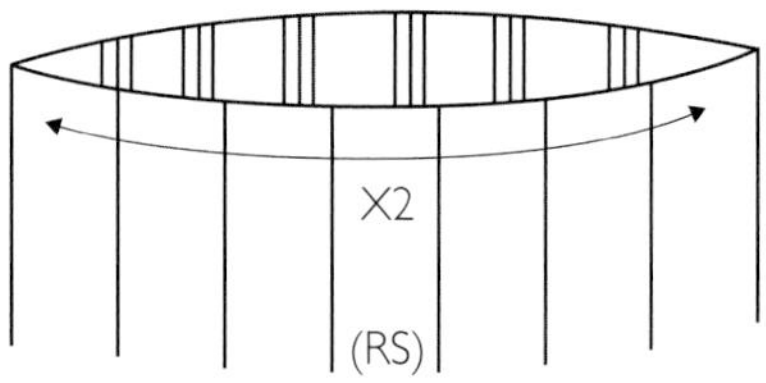

Top of skirt

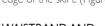

X2

(RS)

Figure 11

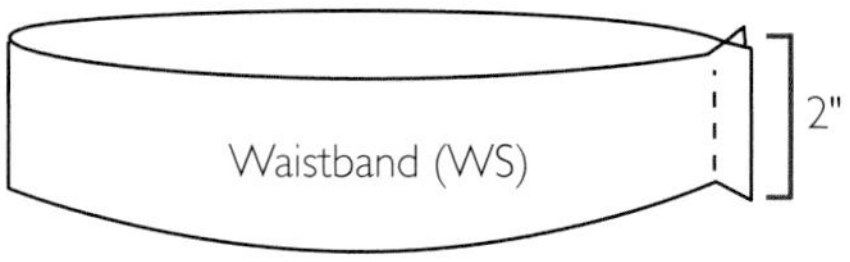

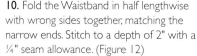

Waistband (WS)

2"

Figure 12

5. Repeat steps 1 through 4 for the remaining Short and Long Godets and Skirt Panels until the skirt has been sewn completely together. Be sure to alternate between the Long and Short Godets as the skirt is being sewn together.

6. Once all of the Panels and Godets have been sewn together, edgestitch on either side of the seams, starting at the upper edge of the skirt. (Figure 10)

WAISTBAND AND INSERTING ELASTIC

7. Measure across the top edge of the skirt front and multiply by 2. This is the size of the opening for the Waistband. Add ½" to this measurement for seam allowance. (Figure 11)

8. Cut a strip from the main fabric (A), 4" wide by the length specified in step 7.

9. It may be necessary to piece more than one 4"-wide strip to get the Waistband length needed. Piece the strips right sides together with a ¼" seam allowance and press the seam open, then trim the strip unit down to the length needed as determined in step 7.

10. Fold the Waistband in half lengthwise with wrong sides together, matching the narrow ends. Stitch to a depth of 2" with a ¼" seam allowance. (Figure 12)

Waistband (RS)

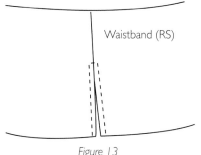

Figure 13

11. Press the seam open and continue pressing back the ¼" seam allowance along the raw edges below the seam.

12. Edgestitch the pressed-under edges to hold them in place. This forms the opening for the insertion of the elastic in steps 19 and 20. (Figure 13)

13. Fold the Waistband widthwise, wrong sides together, and press.

14. With right sides together, pin the Waistband to the upper edge of the skirt with the opening of the Waistband facing away from the skirt, as shown. Stitch with a ½" seam allowance. (Figure 14)

15. Trim or serge the seam, then open out the Waistband away from the skirt and press the seam toward the skirt. Edgestitch along the seamline on the top of the skirt portion.

16. To make the casings in the Waistband (for the elastic), stitch ½" and 1" down from the upper folded edge of the Waistband. This will form 3 casing rows. (Figure 15)

17. Determine where you would like your skirt to rest on your body (at or slightly below natural waistline). Measure around the part of your body where you want the skirt to rest and add 10" (the extra length allows for adjustment later).

18. Cut all three pieces of elastic to the length determined in step 17.

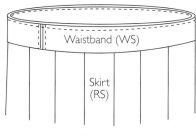

Waistband (WS)

Skirt (RS)

Figure 14

19. Using a safety pin or bodkin, insert the first row of elastic by entering one of the openings in the casing on the wrong side of the Waistband. Continue feeding the elastic through, watching the other end of elastic so that it does not slip into the casing. Leave about 2" to 3" extending from the opening and pin in place at each end.

20. Insert the remaining elastic pieces in the same manner into the other two Waistband casings. Keep the ends of the elastic that are extending outside the openings even. Pin all of them in place from the outside of the skirt to hold them in place.

21. Try on the skirt and make adjustments in the elastic, if needed. Remember to adjust each of them to exactly the same length so that none of the rows appear wavy, indicating that you have one row tighter than another.

22. Once you are happy with the fit, trim away the excess elastic from each end, but leave an extra ½" for overlapping and stitching (in step 23).

23. Taking care not to twist the elastic, gently pull out each end of the elastic away from the skirt and top casing and overlap the ends of the elastic by ½"; stitch the ends together with a zigzag stitch at each elastic end, as shown. (Figure 16) Repeat for the elastic in the remaining two casings.

24. Pull on the Waistband so the stitched ends of the elastic go inside the casings. If desired, stitch down the width of the Waistband through the elastic to keep it from twisting during use.

25. Gently press intentional creases into the top of the skirt and Waistband for a flattering, flat fit.

HEM BAND

26. Cut a series of 2"-wide bias strips from Fabric D. Piece them right sides together with a ¼" seam allowance until you have enough to go around the bottom edge of the skirt plus 2 to 3". This bias strip is your Hem Band. (See Making a Bias Strip on page 141 for more details.)

27. Cut one angled end of the strip straight, then fold that straight-cut end ½" to the wrong side and press. (Figure 17)

28. With wrong sides together, fold the whole strip unit in half along its length and press.

29. Add the Hem Band to the right side of the bottom of the skirt, starting with the pressed-under end of the band. Begin stitching about 2" away from the folded end of the Hem Band and use a ½" seam allowance. (See Applying the Bias Binding Strip on page 141 for more details.)

30. Continue stitching the Hem Band around the bottom of the skirt until the pressed-under end is reached. Allow for

about 1" overlap and trim away any excess Hem Band beyond that. Open out the pressed-under end and tuck the cut end inside it. Finish the band by stitching the tucked-in end in place. (Figure 18)

31. Trim down or serge the Hem Band/skirt seam, then open out the Hem Band away from the skirt and press the seam toward the skirt.

32. Edgestitch the seam on top of the skirt, then edgestitch the lower folded edge of the Hem Band to finish. ❤

TIP
Ideas for Changing Up the Look
If you would like to change the look of the skirt, try some of these ideas:

• Make the whole skirt from one fabric
• Think about making all of the Godets the same height instead of alternating heights
• Make all the Godets from one contrasting fabric

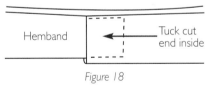

Hemband — Tuck cut end inside

Figure 18

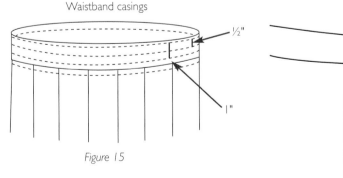

Waistband casings

½"

1"

Figure 15

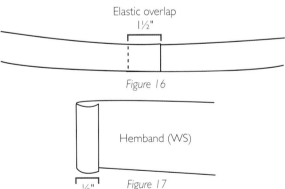

Elastic overlap
1½"

Figure 16

Hemband (WS)

½"

Figure 17

 SWEETWATER

Love Letters Quilt

A Valentine's Day card blown up into a quilt! Featuring red, pink, and white hearts, this sweet and cheery quilt is one you'll want to keep close to your own heart.

FINISHED DIMENSIONS
35 ½" × 35 ½"

FABRIC
• 2¾ yards cream quilting cotton (A) for the Block Background (Moda's 5493-12 Cream used in the sample)
• 1 fat eighth (9" × 20") of each of 10 different coordinating red and cream prints (B) for the Hearts (the following Moda fabrics used in the sample):
  5498-31 Cream Apple Red, 5491-11 Apple Red, 5497-21 Apple Red, 5495-11 Apple Red, 5492-21 Apple Red, 5492-11 Cream Apple Red, 5493-31 Apple Red, 5494-21 Apple Red, and 5496-11 Cream Apple Red
• ⅙ yard coordinating red and cream quilting cotton (B) for Inner Border (Moda *5498-31 Cream Apple Red* used in the sample)
• ¾ yard red and cream quilting cotton (C) for Outer Border and Binding (Moda *5493-31 Apple Red* used in the sample)
• 1¼ yards solid red quilting cotton (D) for Backing (Moda *5455-12* used in the sample)

SUPPLIES
• General Sewing Supplies (page 138)
• Rotary cutter and cutting mat
• 40" × 40 square of batting
• 1½ yards 17"-wide fusible web
• Embroidery floss in cream
• Embroidery needle
• Safety pins (optional)

CUTTING THE FABRIC
1. BLOCK BACKGROUND
Cut thirty-five 5" × 5" squares from cream fabric A.
Cut one square 5" × 5" from solid red fabric D.

2. INNER BORDER
Cut 2 strips 1¼" × 27½" (to sew to the sides of the Block Background).
Cut 2 strips 1¼" × 29" (to sew to the top and bottom of the Block Background).

3. OUTER BORDER
Cut 2 strips 3¾" × 29"—sew to the sides of the quilt.
Cut 2 strips 3¾" × 36 ½"—sew to the top and bottom of the quilt.

4. BACKING
Cut one 40" × 40" Backing square from red fabric D.

5. BINDING
Cut four 2¼" × width of the fabric strips from fabric C.

SEWING INSTRUCTIONS
Sew all seams with right sides together using a ¼" seam allowance unless otherwise noted.

HEART APPLIQUÉS
The Heart Appliqué Template is on a pattern sheet included with this book.

1. Trace around the Heart Template on the paper side of the fusible web 36 times.

2. Following the manufacturer's instructions, fuse the fusible web to the wrong side of each of the 10 fat quarter prints for the Hearts. Trace around the Heart Template on the paper side of the fusible web 35 times.

PLACEMENT DIAGRAM

Make at least three tracings on each of the 10 prints, adding a fourth tracing on five of them. Cut out on traced lines.

2. Make 1 Heart from the background fabric the way you made the other 35.

3. Peel off the paper backing. Following manufacturer's instructions, fuse the red Hearts to the right side of the cream background squares and the cream Heart to the red solid square.

4. Using three strands of cream embroidery floss, sew a blanket stitch (page 140) around the edges of each Heart.

PIECING ROWS

5. With right sides together sew 6 blocks together to make one row, positioning the cream Heart on red Block second block from the right in its row. Make sure the hearts are all oriented in the same direction. You will end up with 6 strips of 6 joined blocks.

6. Piece the 6 strips together along their long edges to form the quilt Block. Position the cream Heart on red strip so the cream Heart is the 2nd row from the bottom.

BORDERS

7. With right sides together and raw edges aligned, stitch the two 1¼" × 27½" Inner Border (B) strips to each side of the quilt Block and the two 1¼" × 29" Inner Border strips to the top and bottom of the quilt Block.

8. With right sides together and raw edges aligned, stitch the two 3¾" × 29" Outer Border strips to the unfinished edges of the side Inner Border strips and the two 3¾" × 36½" Outer Border strips to the top and bottom Inner Border strips. This is the Quilt Top.

BACKING AND BATTING

9. Lay the Backing wrong side up and layer the batting on top of it, aligning raw edges. Center the Quilt Top, right side up, on top of the batting. Baste or safety pin all layers together to hold them stable.

10. Quilt as desired; trim all edges even.

BINDING

11. With right sides together, stitch the short ends of the Binding strips together to make one long strip. Fold it in half lengthwise with wrong sides together and press. Attach the binding (page 141) to the perimeter. ❤

Drawstring Dress

This patterned rose and cream dress features a drawstring neckline, shoulder slits, and elastic cuffs. It looks great when paired with a high-waist belt or worn free!

AMY BUTLER
We carry many of Amy's fabrics, including her wildly popular *Gypsy Caravan*, so we knew *Sew Red* wouldn't be complete without a vintage-inspired garment from Amy, who lost her grandparents to the silent killer. She's been honing her skills in fashion and surface design since she was seven years old, and while she spends much of her time focusing on sewing and designing fabric, she also makes time to take good care of herself through diet, exercise, and managing her mind. Amy has an overwhelming positive energy that's contagious, and we're willing to bet this comes from her IntenSati workout, a mix of interval training and positive affirmations designed to balance your mind and body. She eats several small meals throughout the day, which give her mini breaks from her work table and help keep her mind and creativity fresh.

 AMY'S TIP
Every day, set 5–10 minutes aside to meditate. Stress can take quite a toll on our ticker. Calm the mind, relax the senses, and connect with your inner thoughts.

FINISHED DIMENSIONS
Small fits bust size 34 ½" (6–8)
Medium fits bust size 36" (10–12)
Large fits bust size 39" (14–16)
Finished length 50" (for all sizes)

FABRIC
• 2 yards of quilter's cotton or voile for the main fabric for any size dress (Lark *Ivory/Souvenir pwab068* by Amy Butler for Rowan *Quilting & Style Collection* used in the sample)
• 1½ yards of solid white voile or batiste for the lining for any size dress (any solid white voile or batiste will work for the lining)

SUPPLIES
• General Sewing Supplies (page 138)
• 1 spool of coordinating all-purpose thread
• 1 spool of elastic thread for your sewing machine bobbin
• ¾ yard of ¼" elastic
• Ruler
• Fabric marking pen or pencil
• Safety pin

CUTTING THE FABRIC
CUTTING THE DRESS
1. Use your ruler and marking pen/pencil to mark the measurements for your Dress size directly on the fabric (Figure 1). Cut 2, a Dress Front and a Dress Back.

2. Use the Front and Back you just cut as patterns and cut a Front and Back Lining. Trim the Lining pieces 1" shorter than the Dress along the bottom edge.
NOTE: The finished dress length is 50". To lengthen or shorten your dress, make

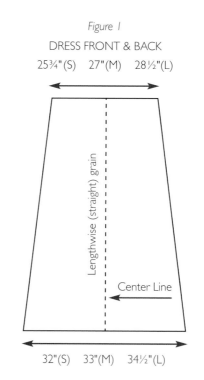

Figure 1
DRESS FRONT & BACK
25¾"(S)   27"(M)   28½"(L)

Lengthwise (straight) grain

Center Line

32"(S)   33"(M)   34½"(L)

adjustments at the hemline. There is a 1" hem included in the 46" length measurement in Figure 1.

3. Use the Armhole Curve Template (on a pattern sheet included with this book) in your size to mark and cut an armhole curve out of both top corners of the Front and Back Dress and Lining pieces. (Figure 2) Set these aside for now.

CUTTING THE SLEEVES
1. Use your ruler and marking pen/pencil to mark the measurements for your Sleeve size directly on the fabric. (Figure 3) Cut 2.

Figure 2

Top Corners

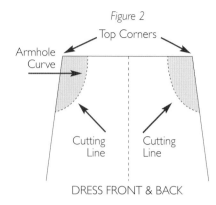

Armhole Curve

Cutting Line | Cutting Line

DRESS FRONT & BACK

Figure 3

Top Corners

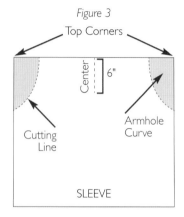

Center | 6"

Cutting Line

Armhole Curve

SLEEVE

Figure 4

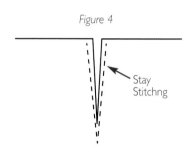

Stay Stitchng

Figure 5

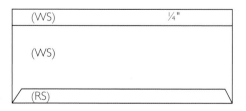

(WS) | ¼"

(WS)

(RS)

2. As you did for the dress, use the Armhole Curve Template to mark and cut two armhole curves at the top corners of each Sleeve. (Figure 3)

CUTTING THE SLEEVE FACINGS

1. Measure the new width at the top of your Sleeve and use a ruler to mark it on the crosswise grain of your Lining fabric. Draw a parallel line of the same length 2⅛" above or below the first line. Draw perpendicular lines at each end. Cut 2 strips.

2. Fold each strip in half by bringing the short ends together and cut in half. You should now have 4 pieces 2⅛" × half the top Sleeve-width measurement. These will be used as your Sleeve Facings. Set them aside for now.

SEWING INSTRUCTIONS

Sew all seams with right sides together, using a ½" seam allowance, unless otherwise indicated. Backstitch at the beginning and end of each seam.

CONTINUOUS BOUND PLACKET ON SLEEVE OPENING

1. Find the center (halfway) point at the top of the Sleeve by folding the Sleeve in half lengthwise and making a snip at the top fold. Open the Sleeve flat and, using your ruler and fabric marker, draw a 6" line down from this center point, perpendicular to the top edge. (Figure 3) Using your scissors, cut along this line. Repeat on the second Sleeve.

2. Reinforce the slit with stay stitching ¼" from the cut edge and tapering down to the bottom. Pivot at this point and then stitch back up the other side to within ¼" of the opposite cut edge. (Figure 4) Repeat on the second Sleeve.

3. To make 2 fabric binding pieces, measure and mark a 1¼"-wide (crosswise grain) × 12"-long (lengthwise grain) rectangle directly on your fabric. Cut 2.

4. Lay each binding piece on your ironing board wrong side up and press ¼" in along one long edge. (Figure 5) Using a fabric marker and ruler, mark a line parallel to and ¼" below the opposite long edge. (Figure 5) Repeat on the other binding.

5. Spread the 6" slit of one Sleeve open and, with right sides together, pin the slit to the marked long edge of one binding strip, aligning the long edges. Position the stay stitching along the slit so it matches the ¼" marked line on the binding piece. Stitch with the slit side facing up and then press. (Figure 6)

6. Bring the folded long edge of the binding over the ¼" seam to the wrong side of the opening and have it extend slightly past the stitching line. Pin from the right side and then machine stitch in place. (Figure 7) Press smooth. Repeat with second Sleeve.

7. Sew the Sleeve seams and press the seam allowance to one side.

SLEEVE HEMS

8. For the sleeve hems, turn up ½" to the wrong side along the bottom edge of each Sleeve. Then turn up again ⅝" to make the casing for the elastic.

9. Stitch completely around the sleeve bottom ½" away from the bottom folded edge, leaving a small (¾") section unstitched as an opening for inserting your elastic. (Figure 8)

Figure 6

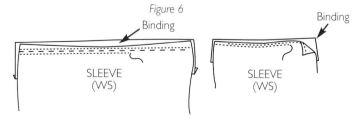

Binding

SLEEVE (WS)

Binding

SLEEVE (WS)

10. Cut 2 pieces of elastic following these measurements: Small – 11³/₈", Medium –12", Large – 12⁷/₈".

11. Using a safety pin attached to one end of the elastic, insert the elastic into the opening of the casing and use the safety pin to feed it through the length of the casing. When it comes back through the opening, cross the two elastic ends on top of each other and bar tack them together. Go back and machine stitch the opening in the casing closed.

SLEEVE FACINGS

12. Take the 4 Sleeve Facing sections you set aside earlier, and on one short end of each, turn in ½" to the wrong side and press.

13. With right sides together, pin the Sleeve Facings to the tops of each Sleeve with the folded end of the facing lined up with the finished edge of the bound plackets at the top of the sleeve, and the other (raw) end lined up even with the top of the armhole curve.

14. Sew the facing to the armhole curve with a ½" seam. Begin ½" in from the end of the armhole curve, take a few stitches, backstitch, and then sew across the top of the Sleeve until you get to the placket and backstitch again. Start again on the other side of the placket, backstitch and continue sewing until you are ½" from the opposite armhole curve. (Figure 9) Press.

15. Repeat with the remaining Sleeve Facings on the other Sleeve.

SEWING THE DRESS

16. Sew the Front to the Back of the Dress at the side seams. Press the seam allowances to one side.

17. Repeat with the Front and Back Lining pieces. Press the seam allowances to one side.

18. Pin the Sleeves to the Dress, matching the underarm curves and the side seams

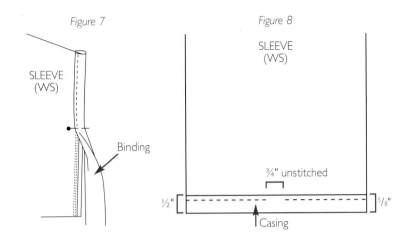

Figure 7

SLEEVE (WS)

Binding

Figure 8

SLEEVE (WS)

¾" unstitched

½"   ⁵/₈"

Casing

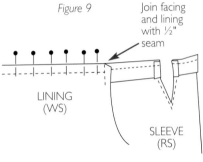

Figure 9

Join facing and lining with ½" seam

LINING (WS)

SLEEVE (RS)

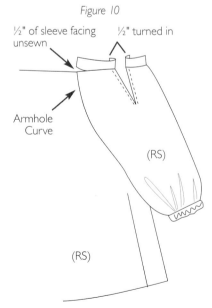

Figure 10

½" of sleeve facing unsewn   ½" turned in

Armhole Curve

(RS)

(RS)

of the Dress with the Sleeve seams. Stitch along the curve, keeping the Sleeve Facings free from any stitching.

19. With the Lining wrong side out and the Dress right side out, slip the Dress into the Lining, matching the top edges of the Front and Back Dress and Lining pieces, and pin them together.

20. Before stitching the Dress and Lining together at the top, turn back the Sleeve Facings to the right sides of the Sleeves and match the short, unstitched ends with the top of the Lining at the seam where the Dress and Sleeve meet. Stitch them together and press the seam allowance toward the Lining. (Figure 10)

21. Sew the Dress and the Lining together along the top edges, meeting up at the point where the Sleeve Facings and the Sleeves are stitched together. (Figure 9) Press these seams open.

22. Turn the Lining to the inside of the Dress and then press it flat along the top edge.

23. Tack the armhole seams of both the Lining and the Dress together either by hand or by machine.

24. Keep the Dress right side out (with Lining inside) and pin again along the top edge of the Dress where you just pressed (step 22) to hold the Lining and the Dress together and to prepare for making the drawstring casing.

25. Make the drawstring casings at the top of the Dress. With the right side of the Dress facing up, start stitching around the

top of the dress, ¾" down from the top edge, beginning at one of the Sleeve openings. Stitch across the Front of the Dress to the other Sleeve opening, catching the Lining and the Sleeve Facings in the stitching. Sew a second row of stitching ¼" down from the first row. This should secure the bottom edges of the Sleeve Facings on the insides of the Sleeves. (Figure 11) Repeat on the Back of the Dress and press.

SMOCKING THE DRESS
26. Using your ruler and a marking pen, draw 6 lines starting ¼" below and parallel to the last stitching line for your casing. The lines should be drawn ¼" apart on both the Front and the Back of the Dress. They should start and stop at the Sleeve seams. (Figure 11)

27. Hand-wind your elastic thread on an empty bobbin, applying a very gentle stretch to the elastic and winding in the same direction as your machine winds your bobbin thread. Put the bobbin in your machine or bobbin case and thread it as usual. Set your machine at a stitch length of 3.0 or longer. Keep your top thread threaded as normal and pull your elastic thread up through the throat plate.

28. With the right side of the dress facing up, backstitch and then slowly stitch across the first marked line. The elastic thread will

stretch as it sews and create a smocked look across the front of the dress. Backstitch when you reach the end of the line. Repeat with the remaining lines.

29. When you are finished smocking, change back to your regular stitch length and all-purpose thread in your bobbin.

FINISHING THE DRESS
30. To make the 2 Drawstrings, measure and mark 2 strips 1¼" (crosswise grain) x 54" (lengthwise grain) out of the remaining fabric and cut them out. Fold each strip in half lengthwise, wrong sides together, and press a crease along the folded edge. Open each strip and then fold each long edge in toward this center crease and press.

31. Fold the strips in half again at the center crease enclosing the raw edges and press. Pin along the matched edges and then edge stitch down both long edges.

32. You will then have 2 drawstrings approximately ¼" wide x 54" long.

33. Using your safety pin, feed the drawstrings through the openings in the Front and Back casings. You can make a small knot at the end of each drawstring. The drawstrings will tie together at the shoulder.

34. To make the hems on the Dress and the Lining, turn up 1" along the bottom edges to wrong sides and press. Then tuck the raw edges of the hems in to the pressed crease to make a ⅝" hem. Topstitch close to the top pressed fold. ♥

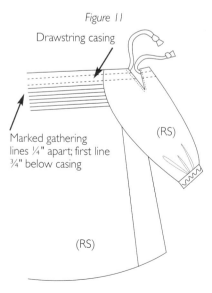

Figure 11

Drawstring casing

(RS)

Marked gathering lines ¼" apart; first line ¾" below casing

(RS)

Target Practice Belt

Show off your embroidery skills with this one-of-a-kind belt! Featuring embroidery detailing over cream linen, the belt ties with a big red bow. It's the perfect accessory to make your outfit pop.

FINISHED DIMENSIONS

Belt panel: 14" × 3¾"
Embroidered center panel: 8¼" × 3¾"
Sash: 3½" × 100"

FABRIC

- 1 fat quarter (18" × 22") linen fabric (A)* in cream for the front and back Belt Center Panel and for the Belt Side Panels (Free Spirit's *Linen Solids* in Butter used in the sample)
- ½ yard solid cotton woven fabric (B) in red for the Binding and Sash Guide (Free Spirit's *Quilting Solids* in Red and Scarlet used in the sample)
- ¼ yard of voile fabric (C) in red for the the Sash (Free Spirit's *Voile Solids* in Tangerine used in the sample)
- *Make sure you can see through the Belt Center Panel fabric (A) either at a light table or at a window to facilitate tracing the embroidery design.

Yardages are based on 45"-wide fabric; adjust as needed.

SUPPLIES

- General Sewing Supplies (page 138)
- ¼ yard medium-weight interfacing
- 1 skein crewel wool in red (Appleton's Crewel Wool, single strand, used in the sample)
- 1 embroidery needle
- Embroidery hoop
- 1 spool coordinating all-purpose thread

CUTTING THE FABRIC

The two Templates are on a pattern sheet included with the book.

1. From the cream linen fabric (A), cut two Belt Side Panels (two for the front and two for the back). Also cut one 12" square for the two Belt Center Panels (one front and one back). Follow steps 1–4 in the Sewing Instructions to trace the Template and transfer the embroidery design to the square and embroider the design. After the design is embroidered, you can then cut out the front and back Belt Center Panels along the cutting lines.

2. From the interfacing, cut one Belt Center Panel and two Belt Side Panels.

3. From the red cotton fabric (B), cut enough 2"-wide bias strips to total 32" in length when stitched together at their short ends for the Binding.

4. From the red cotton voile (C), cut 4 Sash Guides and two 4" × 30" strips for the Sash.

SEWING INSTRUCTIONS

All seams are sewn with right sides together and ¼" seam allowances unless otherwise indicated. Backstitch at the beginning and end of each seam.

EMBROIDERING THE FRONT BELT CENTER PANEL

1. Embroider the design onto the front of the Belt Center Panel. Carefully press and smooth the fabric, then use the Template to trace two Belt Center Panels (front and back) and the embroidery design onto the 12" square of fabric A.

2. Place the traced fabric square in an embroidery hoop and stretch the fabric gently in all directions before tightening the screw to secure the fabric in place.

3. Begin your embroidery in the center of the design and work your way out, using the embroidery stitches indicated on the diagram (or use your own favorite embroidery stitches).

4. Once your embroidery is complete, lay the square right side down onto a clean plush towel and lay a pressing cloth (or a piece of muslin) over the wrong side of the embroidery and steam press it to smooth the fabric and set the stitches. Your front (embroidered) and back Belt Center Panels can now be cut out.

> **♥ TIP**
> Never allow the hot iron to come into direct contact with the wool embroidery. Always use a pressing cloth.

PREPARING AND ASSEMBLING THE BELT

5. With all edges aligned, baste the Belt Center Panel interfacing to the wrong side of the back Belt Center Panel.

6. With all edges aligned, baste a Belt Side Panel interfacing piece to the wrong side of one Belt Side Panel. Repeat on another Belt Side Panel.

7. Place two of the Sash Guides (one with interfacing, one without) wrong sides together and mark the vertical center line. Stitch down the center line from the top for ¾". Repeat stitching along the center line ¾" up from the bottom.

8. Work with one Sash Guide at a time. Fold the top layer of fabric in half along the ¾"-long seam and the marked center line with wrong sides together; press. Repeat on the bottom layer of fabric. You will now have a Sash Guide with the fabric right side out and an opening between the two ¾"-long seams. Repeat Steps 7 and 8 with the remaining front and back Sash Guides.

9. Stitch together the 2"-wide bias strips for the Binding to make a 2" × 32" strip of Binding (pages 140–141). Fold the bias strip in half lengthwise and press, taking care to not stretch the fabric.

10. Read the following assembly instructions to first lay out all the pieces in the order of assembly before sewing.

11. Align one long side edge of one of the Sash Guides with one side edge of the Back Belt Center Panel. Separate the two layers of the Sash Guide and pin one layer only to the Back Belt Center Panel and stitch together using a ¼" seam allowance, keeping the other layer of the Sash Guide free.

12. Repeat step 11 with the remaining Belt Sash at the other side edge of the Back Belt Center Panel.

13. Press the Sash Guides and seam allowances from toward the Sash Guides.

14. Lay the Back Belt Center Panel so that it's facing you. Align the back side of one of the Belt Side Panels onto the outer edge of one layer of the Sash Guide and sew together using a ¼" seam allowance.

Take care to only include the Belt Side Panel and the one layer of the Sash Guide that is facing you in this seam, keeping the other Sash Guide layer free.

15. Repeat step 14 with the remaining Belt Side Panel at the other outer edge of the Sash Guide. Press all seam allowances toward the Sash Guide.

16. Lay the joined belt pieces so that the Front Belt Center Panel is facing you. The unsewn side edges of the Belt Sashes (there are four of them) need to be folded back toward their wrong side by about ¼" and pressed. This will prepare them to be topstitched down onto the Front Belt Center Panel and the Belt Side Panels, thereby hiding the seam allowances of the belt construction.

17. Topstitch through all layers a scant ⅛" from each edge of each Sash Guide. Press well.

FINISHING THE BELT AND SASH

18. Apply the bias Binding strip you made in step 9 to the perimeter of the Belt, mitering all corners.

19. With right sides together, stich the two 4" × 30" Sash strips at the short ends, making a 4" × 60" length. Press the seam open. Hand or machine stitch a ¼" rolled hem around all raw edges of the Sash. Cut the ends of the Sash at an angle before hemming if desired. Press and thread the Sash through the Sash Guides. ♥

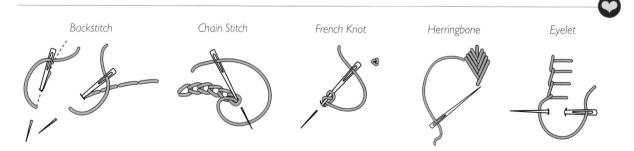

| Backstitch | Chain Stitch | French Knot | Herringbone | Eyelet |

❤ **MARCIA HARMENING**

Queen of Hearts

Straight out of Wonderland, the Queen of Hearts will be wondering what you're doing with her quilt! This fantastical design allows you to use your favorite appliqué technique.

FINISHED DIMENSIONS
24½" × 24½"

FABRIC
The fabrics used for the quilt front are all from Free Spirit Fabrics.

- 1 yard quilting cotton in red (A) for the Center Motif and Corner Triangles (*DB B11 Red Designer Beads* used in the sample)
- ¾ yard quilting cotton in white (B) for the Center Block and Corner Motif (*DS S28 Arctic White* used in the sample)
- 1 yard quilting cotton in black (C) for the Center and Corner Motifs, the Flange, and the Binding (*DS S12 Black* used in the sample)
- ⅞ yard quilting cotton in a coordinating color (D) for the Backing (*DS S61 True Red* used in the sample)

Yardages are based on 45"-wide fabric; adjust as needed.

SUPPLIES
- General Sewing Supplies (page 138)
- 28" × 28" piece of batting
- Rotary cutter and cutting mat
- Red, white, and black lightweight thread for hand or machine appliqué (the sample was appliquéd by hand)
  or
- Fusible web and nylon thread for raw-edge fusible appliqué
- Safety pins (optional)

CUTTING THE FABRIC
1. WHITE FABRIC (B) FOR THE CENTER BLOCK
Cut one 18" × 18" square (will trim to 16½" × 16 ½" after appliqué is complete).

2. RED FABRIC (A) FOR THE CORNERS
Cut two 14" × 14" squares.

3. BLACK FABRIC (C)
For the Flange: Cut four ¾" × 16½" rectangles.
For the Binding: Cut three strips 2¼" by the width of the fabric.

4. BACKING FABRIC (D)
Cut one 28" × 28" square.

MARCIA HARMENING
Marcia, a mom and the owner/designer of Happy Stash Quilts, recently moved to Reno, Nevada, and made a stop at our local store to browse our new fabric section. It must have been fate, because the very afternoon that she walked into Jimmy Beans Wool, we were looking for designers to be a part of *Sew Red*. Talk about being in the right place at the right time! Little did we know then that when Marcia's father was just 50, he suffered his first heart attack; 10 years later he underwent quadruple bypass open-heart surgery. Watching her father's health drastically improve through exercise, dietary changes, and weight loss has been a major motivating factor for Marcia. She makes sure to work out before becoming consumed by a project. Morning walks and afternoon Zumba classes get her heart racing!

❤ **MARCIA'S TIP**
Marcia aspires to be like her grandma and encourages us to find both short-term and long-term goals. "Today I walk one mile. Two months from now, I will walk in a 5K race. Fifty years from now, I'll be like my 90-year-old grandma."

CUTTING CHART FOR APPLIQUÉ PIECES

	A	B	B-r	C	C-r	D	D-r	E	E-r	F	F-r	G	H	I	J	K	L	M	N	O	O-r
Black	4	8	8	4	4	4	4	4	4	4	4	4	4	8	48	8	12	12	5	4	4
Red	4	4	4	4	4	4	4	4	4	4	4	4	4	4	24	4	4	4	1	4	4
White		4	4											4	24	4	8	8	4		

The Templates for the Queen of Hearts Center motif and the Queen of Hearts Corner motif are on a pattern sheet included with this book.

1. Using the Templates, cut the number of Appliqué pieces listed for each shape in the designated fabric color. All black fabric pieces will be slightly larger than the red and white pieces.

2. Cut each of the two 14" squares (A) in half diagonally to create the four Red Corners.

SEWING INSTRUCTIONS

All seams are sewn right sides together using a ¼" seam allowance unless otherwise indicated. Backstitch at the beginning and end of each seam.

APPLIQUÉ

The "Shadow Pop" effect in this wall hanging is created by appliquéing each piece in the motif twice. The solid lines on the diagrams indicate the larger black pieces, which are appliquéd first. The dashed lines on the diagrams indicate the slightly smaller red and white pieces, which are appliquéd on top of the black pieces.

TIP
Sew the appliqué pieces to the backgrounds in alphabetical order of color—black fabric first and then the red or white fabric piece for each letter on the chart.

1. Select your favorite method of appliqué (see below) and complete the Center Block and all four Corners. Applique the Red and Black Center Motif pieces on the 18" x 18" White Center Block and the White and Black Corner Motif pieces on the Red Corners.

Fusible Web:

If you are using fusible web for a raw-edge appliqué, trace the appliqué shapes onto the fusible web at the size they are drawn. (Trace the solid lines for all black appliqué pieces and trace the dashed lines for all red and white appliqué pieces, following the diagrams.)

Hand or Machine Appliqué:

If you are turning the edges of your pieces for hand or machine appliqué, then add a ⅛" to ¼" seam allowance to all cut pieces for turning the edges under on each piece.

2. Once the appliqué process is complete, press the Center Block and four Corners.

SEWING THE WALL HANGING TOP AND BACKING

3. With wrong sides together, press each of the four ¾" x 16½" Black Flange rectangles in half lengthwise.

4. Trim the Center Block to a 16½" x 16½" square.

5. With right sides together, align the raw edges of the four black Flange pieces (B) with the four raw edges of the White Center Block and staystitch them together using a scant ⅛" seam allowance.

6. Center each Corner along each raw edge of the Center Block, with the Flange sandwiched between them, and the raw edges of the Corner, Flange and Center Block aligned. Stitch with a ¼" seam allowance. Press seams flat. This completes the Wall Hanging Top.

7. Lay the Backing (D) wrong side up and place the batting on top, with raw edges aligned. Center the Wall Hanging Top, right side up, on top of the batting, and secure all layers together by basting or with safety pins.

8. With right sides together, stitch the three Black Binding strips (C) for the binding together at their short ends, forming one long strip; press the strip in half lengthwise, with wrong sides together.

9. Quilt as desired; trim all edges even. Apply the Binding (page 141) around the perimeter of the wall hanging. ❤

Center Motif

Corner Motif

♥ KRISTEN ASHBAUGH-HELMREICH

Mobius Cowl Wrap

It's easy to create this simple wrap that can be worn five different ways. Perfect for a first sewing project, it looks great any way you twist it!

FINISHED DIMENSIONS
40" × 42"

FABRIC
• I yard each of two different coordinating 55"-wide cotton voile fabrics (*Bloom* in Mandarin (A) and *Wild Field* in Cherry (B) from Valori Wells's *Wrenly Collection* used in the sample. The cowl can also be made in one fabric, just double the yardage)

SUPPLIES
• General Sewing Supplies (page 138)
• I spool of all-purpose thread (Gutermann 100% Polyester thread in color #405 used in sample)

CUTTING THE FABRIC
1. Cut five 16" (lengthwise grain) × 14" (crosswise grain) pieces each from fabrics A and B (10 pieces total).

SEWING INSTRUCTIONS
All seams are sewn right sides together using a ½" seam allowance unless otherwise indicated. Backstitch at the beginning and end of each seam.

1. With right sides together, make two long fabric strips by sewing the cut pieces together along their 14" edges. Alternate A and B pieces in each strip as follows: Strip 1: A, B, A, B, A and Strip 2: B, A, B, A, B.

2. Check the strip length and shorten both strips equally if desired. Press the seams open.

3. With right sides together, pin and stitch the strips together along the two long edges, aligning the seams of the cut pieces and leaving the short ends open.

4. Press the seams open, then turn the piece right side out and press it flat. Topstitch the long sides ¼" from the edge.

5. Lay the piece flat. Flip one short end over so the fabric twists. Pin the short ends together, aligning the raw edges; the Cowl will be twisted in the center. Stitch the ends together in a French seam as follows: Stitch a ¼" seam; press it to one side. Fold the cowl along this seam so the raw edges are inside the fold. Stitch ⅜" away from the fold, encasing the raw edges within the seam.

6. Press the French seam to one side and topstitch ⅛" from the seam. ♥

KRISTEN ASHBAUGH-HELMREICH
A young, up-and-coming knitwear designer (and now seamstress), Kristen is one of Jimmy Beans Wool's own. She manages all of our social media outlets and is also our in-house designer, cranking out beautiful knits as free patterns for our newsletter. (Her first published knitting design was featured in our book *Knit Red*, released in June 2012.) This design is another first for Kristen; she picked up sewing when we added our fabric department. A Jimmy Beans Wool employee by day and creator of Marinade Designs (all things crafty and homemade) by night, Kristen is one running, knitting, sewing, yoga-practicing bean we couldn't live without! From balanced eating habits to long-distance running, this gal makes sure to take extra good care of her body to offset her predisposition to heart disease.

♥ **KRISTEN'S TIP**
Stay active, eat healthy, and maintain healthy relationships with those you love. These tips alone will keep your ticker going for many happy years.

Tides Coming In

Black and white geometric shapes formed by details in the fabric and the quilt pattern separate red sections and make this quilt resemble tides coming in at the beach.

FINISHED DIMENSIONS
39½" × 32½"

FABRIC
• 1½ yards quilting cotton in cream and black print (A) for small strips and Binding (Free Spirit Designer *Morning Tides*, MC13 Cream used in the sample)
• 3 yards quilting cotton (B–G) in red for larger strips and Backing (Free Spirit Designer *Essential Solid*, S61 True Red used in the sample)

Yardages are based on 45"-wide fabric; adjust as needed.

SUPPLIES
• General Sewing Supplies (page 138)
• 1½ yards batting
• Rotary cutter and cutting mat
• Coordinating all-purpose thread
• Safety pin (optional)

Red fabric (B–G)	Cut piece dimensions	Number of pieces to cut
B	3" × 15"	6
C	3" × 12"	5
D	3" × 18"	5
E	3" × 9"	5
F	3" × 21"	3
G	3" × 6"	3
H	3" × 24"	3
Backing	42" × 36"	1

CUTTING THE FABRIC
1. FABRIC A
Cut 16 pieces, each 3" × 6".

2. BINDING (A)
Cut four 2½" × width of fabric strips.

3. BATTING
Cut 1 piece 42" × 36".

SEWING INSTRUCTIONS
All seams are sewn right sides together using a ¼" seam allowance unless otherwise indicated. Backstitch at the beginning and end of each seam.

1. Sew the vertical (lengthwise) strips together, following the diagram (from left: B to A to B, D to A to C, F to A to E, etc.). You will have a total of 16 strips.

2. Assemble the 16 lengthwise strips together, following the diagram, to finish the Quilt Top.

3. With right sides together, stitch the four Binding strips together at their short ends, forming one long strip; press the strip in half lengthwise, with wrong sides together. Trim the Binding strip to 146" long.

4. Lay the Backing (H) wrong side up and place the batting on top, with raw edges aligned. Center the Quilt Top, right side up, on top of the batting, and secure all layers together by basting or with safety pins.

5. Quilt as desired; trim all edges even. Apply the Binding (page 141) around the perimeter of the quilt. ♥

MARK CESARIK
Mark Cesarik is the Batman of the fabric world: a graphic designer by day, artist and world-class doodler by night (he drew the design for the invitations to his wedding!). Often using his hand-drawn designs to create patterns, Mark has an eye (and hand) for designing irresistible fabrics. He and his wife started Sew Bettie (a collection of kitschy designs), which was featured in *The New York Times*. Mark designs fabric collections for Free Spirit, and in 2011 Jimmy Beans Wool started to carry them. We are fairly certain his line was what started our new fabric addiction. We are in complete awe of his fabrics and had to include him in *Sew Red*. Mark and his wife have a very straightforward take on heart-healthy living: eat healthy and exercise. Hey, no arguments here.

♥ **MARK'S TIP**
"If you haven't gotten your daily exercise in, you can't quilt."
— *Jinny Beyer, well-known quilter*

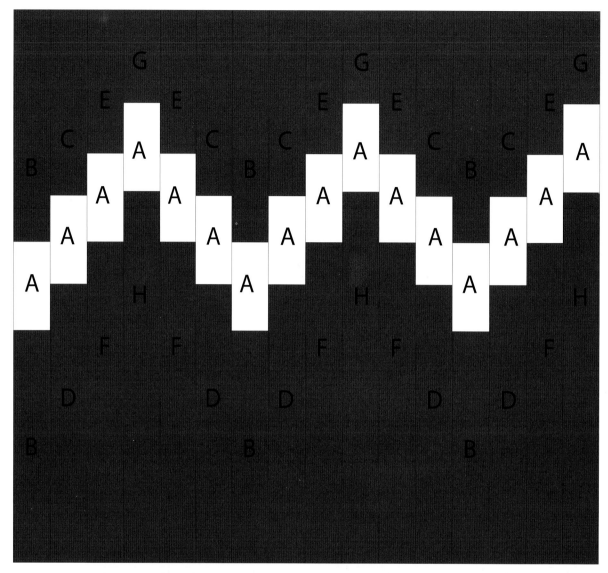

Quilt detail

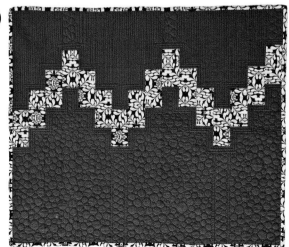

Sonoma Purse

Made from just three fat quarters of fabric, this pleated stripwork purse is big on style! This easy-to-sew little bag will impress even the most discerning of friends.

PATTY YOUNG

Laura met Patty (the face behind MODKID designs) at Quilt Market and immediately knew *Sew Red* wouldn't be complete without a design from this creative gal! Little did we know, Patty experienced the devastating effects of heart disease firsthand. In 1979 Patty's grandmother Mama Alicia passed away from a heart attack while walking home from church in Costa Rica. By the time her neighbor found her and called an ambulance, it was too late to save her. Since then, Patty has taken her grandmother's story to heart and structured her lifestyle around exercise and good eating habits. Her mom actually set the example, frequenting the gym even in her late 60s. By teaching her children to love veggies and heart-healthy proteins like fish, she's showing them the benefits of healthy eating.

FINISHED DIMENSIONS
15" wide × 8" high × 1½" deep with a 21"-long handle.

FABRIC
• 2 fat quarters (22" × 18") of coordinating fabrics (A and B) for Outer Shell (*Sari Wrap Pomegranate* from the *Grand Bazaar* collection and *Tiny Dots Chocolate* from *Andalucia 2012* by Patty Young used in the sample)

• 1 fat quarter of coordinating fabric for Lining (*Tiny Dots Chocolate* from *Andalucia 2012* by Patty Young used in sample) Yardages are based on 45"-wide fabric; adjust as needed.

SUPPLIES
• General Sewing Supplies (page 138)
• 1 yard of lightweight fusible interfacing
• Rotary cutter and cutting mat
• 1 magnetic snap
• Coordinating all-purpose thread
• ⅔ yard of decorative ribbon for purse handle (optional) (*Sari Wrap Pomegranate*
• ⅞" jacquard ribbon, from Patty's *Grand Bazaar* ribbon collection, used in the sample)
• Water-soluble fabric marker
• Ruler
• Thread nippers or embroidery scissors

CUTTING THE FABRIC
1. Cut each Outer Shell fabric (A and B) in half, making four 22" × 9" pieces.

2. From one 22" × 9" piece of fabric A and one of fabric B, cut five 4" × 9" pieces; (10 pieces total) for the Outer Shell Strips.

3. Cut each of the two remaining 22" × 9" pieces (one in fabric A and one in B) in half, making four 22" × 4½" pieces. Set aside one piece of each color for the Interior Pocket and the Purse Handle.

4. Cut each of the two remaining 22" × 4½" pieces in half, making four 22" × 2¼" strips for the Purse Gusset.

5. Don't cut the Lining fabric yet; we'll do that during the sewing process.

♥ **PATTY'S TIP**
Patty firmly believes in a daily dose of laughter! We couldn't agree more; laughter is the best medicine!

Figure 1

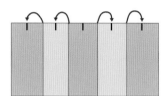

Figure 2

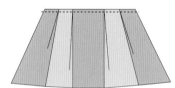

Figure 3

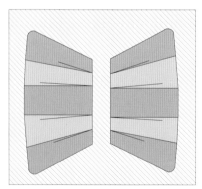

Figure 4

SEWING INSTRUCTIONS

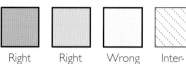

| Right Side A | Right Side B | Wrong Side | Inter-facing |

All seams are sewn right sides together using a ½" seam allowance unless otherwise indicated. Backstitch at the beginning and end of each seam.

1. To make the Outer Shell front and back panels, arrange 5 of the 4" × 9" Outer Shell Strips with the colors alternating. Arrange the remaining Outer Shell Strips in the same way, placing each group opposite the other. (Figure 1)

2. Stitch the first group of 5 strips to each other along their 9" edges. Press the seams to one side. Stitch and press the second group of 5 strips in the same way to make 2 Outer Shell sections. Following manufacturer's directions, fuse lightweight interfacing to the wrong side of each Outer Shell piece.

3. Pleat the Outer Shell pieces as follows: Mark the center of each strip along the top edge, leaving the middle strip unmarked. (Figure 2)

3. Working your way out from the center strip, fold each vertical seam toward the center mark of the adjacent strip and press, creating a ½" pleat. (Figure 2) Repeat for the other side of the piece. There will be four pleats on each Outer Shell piece with the center strip left unpleated. Baste across the top edge to hold all the pleats in place. (Figure 3)

4. To round out the bottom corners of each Outer Shell, trace around a quarter or other small round object. Trim along the marked lines. (Figure 4)

5. Fuse lightweight interfacing to the wrong side of the Lining fabric.

6. Use the Outer Shell pieces as patterns to cut two Lining pieces as follows: Place the Lining fabric wrong side up. Place the Outer Shell pieces right side up on the lining fabric, opening out the pleats at the bottom edge. (Figure 4) Trace along the outer edge of the Outer Shell pieces; cut out the Lining pieces. Mark the center top of each Lining piece and attach the halves of the magnetic snap to each piece, about 1½" down from the top edge, following manufacturer's instructions.

7. To make the Interior Pocket, fold the interior pocket fabric (cut in step 3) in half crosswise with right sides together, making an 11" × 4½" piece. Stitch the open edges, leaving a small opening on one side for turning. (Figure 5) Trim the corners; turn the Pocket right side out and press. Center the Pocket over the right side of one of the lining pieces, close to the bottom so the side edges of the pockets are at least ¾" away from the edge of the lining; pin. Edgestitch the Pocket to the lining along the sides and bottom edge, leaving the top edge unstitched. (Figure 6) Place the lining pieces aside.

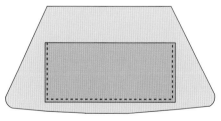

Figure 6

Figure 5

Figure 7

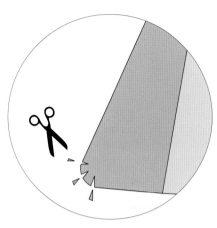

Figure 8

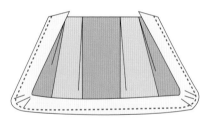

Figure 9

8. Create the purse Gusset (for the sides and bottom) by sewing two matching 22" x 2¼" strips (from Cutting step 4) at one short edge. Trim 4½" from each end, creating a 34" x 2¼" piece for the Outer Gusset. (Figure 7) Make the Lining Gusset from the remaining 22" x 2¼" strips in the same way. Fuse interfacing to wrong side of each gusset strip.

9. Using thread nippers or embroidery scissors, make a series of small wedge cuts along the rounded edges of the Outer Shell pieces to eliminate bulk when attaching the Outer Gusset. (Figure 8) With right sides together, pin the Outer Gusset along the outer edge of one Outer Shell piece. Stitch along the curved edge. (Figure 9) Attach the other Outer Shell piece to the other edge of the Outer Gusset in the same way. Trim the seam allowances to ¼", then turn the Outer Shell right side out.

10. Attach the Lining Gusset to the purse Lining pieces in the same way as for the Outer Shell, but leave a 4" opening along one bottom edge seam for turning the purse right side out later. Leave the Lining inside out.

11. For the Purse Handle, fuse interfacing to the wrong side of the 22" x 4½" Purse Handle piece. Fold it in half lengthwise, with right sides together, then stitch the long edge, leaving the short edges open for turning. (Figure 10) Turn right side out; press. Topstitch 1/8" from both long edges. If desired, embellish the Purse Handle with a decorative stitch or ribbon trim before attaching it to the purse.

12. With right sides together, pin the short ends of the Purse Handle to the raw edges of the Outer Shell Gussets at the top of the purse, making sure not to twist the handle. Baste in place. (Figure 11)

13. Insert the Outer Shell inside the Lining, right sides together, with the Handle sandwiched between the Lining and the Outer Shell. (Figure 12) Pin the top edge, keeping all seams and raw edges aligned. Stitch the upper edge, backstitching along the areas where the Purse Handle ends are basted.

14. Turn the purse right side out through the opening in the bottom seam of the lining. Slipstitch the opening closed, then push the lining into the purse. Topstitch the upper edge of the purse. ♥

Figure 10

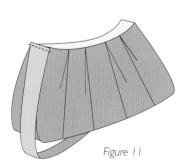

Figure 11

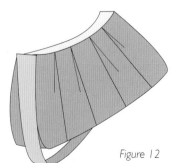

Figure 12

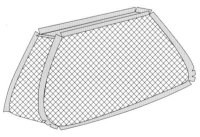

SAREMY DUFFY

Jewelry Case

Black and white and red all over! The rectangular design of this case is a perfect way to show off the fabric's unique bicycle motif. As sturdy and practical as it is fetching.

SAREMY DUFFY
Saremy is the mastermind behind the wildly popular Chicken Boots line of knitting accessories, and we knew we had to have an eye-popping original from her in *Sew Red*. Saremy's mother was a nurse who worked in a heart catheterization lab (which runs diagnostic tests to see if someone is at risk for heart disease), and saw firsthand how devastating the disease can be. Though she was a squeamish kid and spent many afternoons napping in the lab's observation deck while her mother worked, she picked up on heart-healthy eating and exercising habits from her mother's example. Now a mother herself, Saremy and her husband focus on eating organic, local foods and staying active, even though her life consists of lots of sewing! An avid cyclist-turned-runner, Saremy makes it a point to get her morning run in before becoming consumed by work.

FINISHED DIMENSIONS

8¼" tall × 4½" wide when closed
8¼" tall × 9" wide when open

FABRIC

- One fat quarter (18" × 22") of quilting cotton for Outer Case (*Filling in My Flower Basket with Roses* by RubyDoor, www.spoonflower.com, used for sample)
- One fat quarter of coordinating quilting cotton for Lining/Inner Case (quilting cotton used in sample courtesy of Windham Fabrics)
- One fat quarter of a second coordinating quilting cotton for Binding, interior and exterior (*Painter's Canvas* in Red by Laura Gunn used in sample)
- One 5" × 11" piece of a third coordinating quilting cotton for Necklace Holder (*Shirtings 1875–1900 Bicycles* by Terry Clothier for Moda Fabrics used in sample)
- One 5" × 5" piece of wool felt any color for Earring Holders (NOTE: Use wool felt, not craft felt)
- One 4" × 9" piece of clear vinyl or same size piece of fourth quilting cotton (for Zippered and Necklace Pockets)

Yardages are based on 45"-wide fabric; adjust as needed.

SUPPLIES

- General Sewing Supplies (page 138)
- ⅓ yard non-fusible heavyweight interfacing, such as Peltex
- One ½" × 2½" length of hook and loop tape, such as Velcro
- One 5" zipper in coordinating color (for pocket)
- One 34" continuous coil chain zipper length in coordinating color (for case)
- Zipper pull
- All-purpose thread (to match binding fabric and hook and loop tape)
- Screw-punch for holes in Earring Holder OR use an awl or ice pick
- Pinking shears

SAREMY'S TIP
Turn the common "I worked out this morning, so I can eat this brownie" mentality into "I worked hard this morning and deserve to look good in my clothes, so I will not eat that brownie!"

CUTTING THE FABRIC

The pattern for the Outer Case and Lining/Inner Case (A and B) and templates for the Earring (E) and Necklace (F1–F4) Holders are on a pattern sheet included with this book. You will cut the Necklace (C) and Zippered (D) Pockets from measurements.

1. OUTER CASE (A)
Cut one in main fabric on the fold.

2. LINING/INNER CASE (B)
Cut one in contrasting fabric on the fold and one in interfacing fabric on the fold.

3. EARRING HOLDERS (E)
Cut two from wool felt using pinking shears.

4. F1 TO F4 NECKLACE HOLDER (F1–F4)
Cut one each from third contrasting fabric F1: Outside bottom piece; F2: Inside bottom piece (hook tape); F3: Inside top piece (loop tape); F4: Outside top piece.

5. BINDING
Cut several 1⅜"-wide bias strips from second contrasting fabric and join end to end to make a 1⅜" × 60" bias strip.

6. NECKLACE POCKET
Cut one 4" × 4½" piece of vinyl (or contrasting fabric).

7. ZIPPERED POCKET
Cut one 3" × 4½" piece of vinyl (or contrasting fabric).

Transfer all pattern markings to the right side of fabric pieces A/B, E, and F1–F4.

SEWING INSTRUCTIONS

Sew all seams with right sides together using a ¼" seam allowance unless otherwise indicated. Backstitch at the beginning and end of each seam.

1. With right sides together and curved edges aligned, pin then machine stitch F1 and F4 together along the curved edge; press and understitch seam to the longer (F1) piece. (Figure 1) This is the outside layer of the necklace holder.
Following the placement marks, stitch the hook tape to the right side of F2 and the loop tape to the right side of F3. With right sides together and curved edges aligned, stitch F2 to F3 along curved edge; press and understitch seam to the longer (F3) piece. (Figure 2) This is the inside layer.

2. Open the inner and outer holder pieces flat and press. With right sides together (F1 faces F2; F4 faces F3) and all edges matching, pin then stitch together along three sides, leaving the top raw edges (F1 and F3) open for turning. Clip corners, turn right side out and press. Edgestitch around the three seamed edges. (The top raw edges will eventually be stitched to the case perimeter.) (Figure 3)

> **TIP**
> Vinyl can be purchased in most fabric stores; if desired, recycle part of an old vinyl bag, like those used for bed linens. The sample uses 12-gauge vinyl.

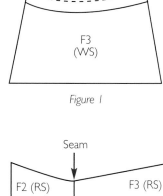

Figure 1

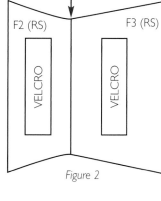

Seam

Figure 2

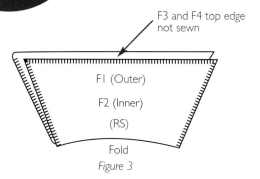

F3 and F4 top edge not sewn

Figure 3

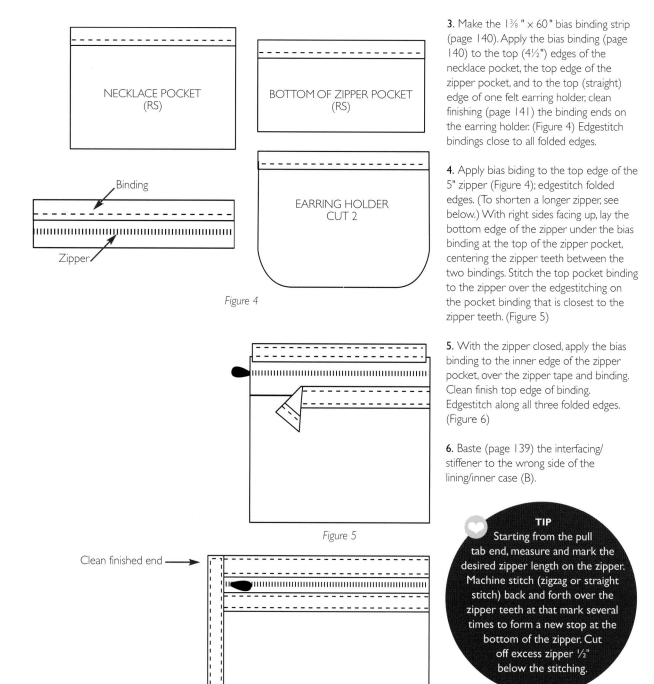

Figure 4

Figure 5

Figure 6

3. Make the 1⅜" × 60" bias binding strip (page 140). Apply the bias binding (page 140) to the top (4½") edges of the necklace pocket, the top edge of the zipper pocket, and to the top (straight) edge of one felt earring holder; clean finishing (page 141) the binding ends on the earring holder. (Figure 4) Edgestitch bindings close to all folded edges.

4. Apply bias biding to the top edge of the 5" zipper (Figure 4); edgestitch folded edges. (To shorten a longer zipper, see below.) With right sides facing up, lay the bottom edge of the zipper under the bias binding at the top of the zipper pocket, centering the zipper teeth between the two bindings. Stitch the top pocket binding to the zipper over the edgestitching on the pocket binding that is closest to the zipper teeth. (Figure 5)

5. With the zipper closed, apply the bias binding to the inner edge of the zipper pocket, over the zipper tape and binding. Clean finish top edge of binding. Edgestitch along all three folded edges. (Figure 6)

6. Baste (page 139) the interfacing/stiffener to the wrong side of the lining/inner case (B).

TIP
Starting from the pull tab end, measure and mark the desired zipper length on the zipper. Machine stitch (zigzag or straight stitch) back and forth over the zipper teeth at that mark several times to form a new stop at the bottom of the zipper. Cut off excess zipper ½" below the stitching.

7. Place the Lining/Inner Case right side up (fabric side up) and place the Necklace Holder (with the top raw edge matching the top raw edge of the lining). Place both felt Earring Holders; the raw edge of unbound holder is placed at the top edge of the lining, and the bound Earring Holder just below. Place the necklace and Zippered Pockets so that the bottom and outside edges align. Place the side binding of the zipper pocket over the unbound side edge of the necklace pocket. Baste the holders and pockets in place through all layers. Stitch the top edge of the Necklace Holder and the top edge of the unbound Earring Holder to the top edge of the lining. For the bound Earring Holder, stitch over the top row of edgestitching on the Binding to secure it to the lining; for the Zippered Pocket, stitch over only the top row of the Binding edgestitching, so you can unzip and access the Pocket. Do not sew the top edge of the Necklace Pocket to the lining. (Figure 7)

8. With wrong sides together, baste the Outer Case (A) to the Lining/Inner Case (B) through all layers. (Note: If your outer case fabric is directional, make sure the design runs in the same direction as the case interior.) Mark the centers at the top and the bottom of the case, where it will fold when zipped closed.

9. The zipper begins and ends at the center bottom, leaving a loose, 2" zipper tail. Mark one end of the 34"-long continuous coil zipper chain 2" from the end. Match that mark to the bottom right marking on the inside case and baste zipper length around the outer edge of the case (zipper teeth inward). Stitch zipper to case, being sure to keep it taut and evenly curved around the case's corners. Stop stitching at the bottom left marking; two 2" lengths of zipper remain loose and unattached at center bottom. (Figure 8)

NOTE: A continuous coil zipper chain has very fine teeth that make it very flexible when sewn around corners and at sharp angles.

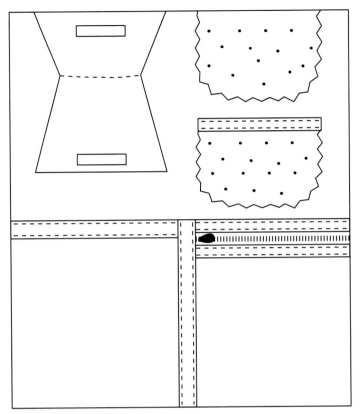

Figure 7

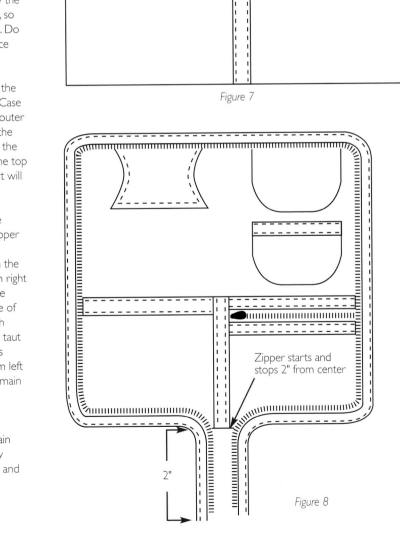

Zipper starts and stops 2" from center

2"

Figure 8

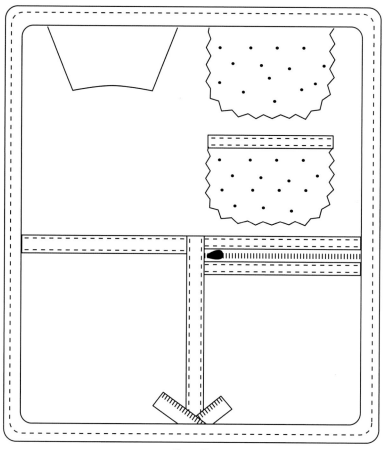

Figure 9

10. Starting at the center bottom on the inside of the case, apply the bias binding over the zipper, being sure to leave the loose zipper end free, as shown. At the corners, be sure to pull the binding taut and keep the seam allowance consistent, as you did with the zipper. (Figure 9)

11. Add the zipper pull to both loose ends of the zipper and close the first ½" or so of the zipper. Apply bias binding over the bottom raw edge of the zipper, stitching over the zipper teeth. (Figure 10 and detail) ♥

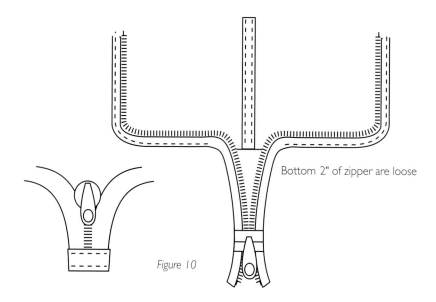

Bottom 2" of zipper are loose

Figure 10

 ANNA COHEN

Petal Dress

Petal perfection! This sweet coral dress is young, fun, and versatile, perfect for day and night. Any girl would be excited to have it in her wardrobe.

FINISHED DIMENSIONS

Size 4 (sample):
Bust 34", Waist 26½", Hips 36"
Size 6:
Bust 35", Waist 27½", Hips 37"
Size 8:
Bust 36", Waist 28½", Hips 38"
Size 10:
Bust 37", Waist 29½", Hips 39"
Size 12:
Bust 38½", Waist 30", Hips 40½"

FABRIC:

- 2½ yards (sizes 4, 6, 8); 2¾ yards (sizes 10, 12) of red wool/silk felted fabric (not craft felt) for the Petals (custom-dyed felted wool/silk fabric, available from Imperial Yarns, used in the sample)
- 2½ yards (sizes 4, 6, 8); 2¾ yards (sizes 10, 12) of heavyweight (40 mm) red silk charmeuse for the Bodice, Bodice Lining, and Skirt Front and Back (*Silk Charmeuse Red* from Exotic Silk used in the sample)
- 2 yards (sizes 4, 6, 8); 2¼ yards (sizes 10, 12) of red silk taffeta forthe Skirt Lining (*Ultra Taffeta Cardinal* from the Signature Series used in the sample)
- 2 yards (sizes 4, 6, 8); 2¼ yards (sizes 10, 12) of fine red tulle for the Underskirt (*Tulle Fine Mesh: American Beauty* from The Spool used in the sample)

SUPPLIES

- General Sewing Supplies (page 138)
- Matching all-purpose thread
- 11" red invisible zipper
- Pattern tracing cloth or tissue paper (optional)

CUTTING THE FABRIC

Pattern pieces **A–G** are on the pattern sheet in envelope inside the back cover of the book.
A: Petals (Row 1)
B: Petals (Row 2)
C: Petals (Row 3)
D: Petals (Row 4)
E: Back Waistband/Yoke
F: Front Waistband/Yoke
G: Bodice Back
H: Bodice Front

ANNA COHEN

This gorgeous dress comes from the collaborative efforts of designer Anna Cohen and Imperial Yarn. Jeanne and Dan own Imperial Stock Ranch, the name behind some truly fabulous designs and yarns. Jeanne knew just the design we needed for Sew Red—this petal dress, originally designed in white as a wedding dress for Emily Powell of Powell's Books. This red version is made from their hand-felted wool fabrics. Between creating extravagant designs, Anna runs a few times a week and attends Zumba classes to keep her ticker in tip-top shape. Fortunately, she does not have a family history of heart disease. As a vegetarian, Anna found she was loading up on simple carbohydrates (like breads, pastas, rice, and corn), which turn straight to sugar and can cause many heart troubles. She has since kicked these foods from her diet (almost entirely) and feels great.

 ANNA'S TIP

Do what you love and follow your heart. It will lead you to inspiration and discovery that will keep you wanting to be awake for the most incredible mystery and adventure that this life is!

Cut the following pieces (I–J) from measurements (no pattern pieces):

I: Skirt
J: Skirt Lining
K: Tulle Underskirt

Lay out the pattern pieces following the lengthwise grainlines marked on them.

Use the pattern pieces A–G themselves, or trace them onto pattern tracing cloth or tissue paper and cut out.

1. From the felted wool fabric, cut each of the four different-sized Petal patterns. They are all cut on the fold. Be sure to cut out the correct size Petals for your size dress. Cut 10 Petals each in each of the four sizes (A, B, C, and D). Transfer all pattern markings to the fabric.

Finish the Edges of each cut Petal:
Wet each Petal in a bowl of warm water with a few of drops of liquid dish soap added. Place the Petal on flat surface and rub the edges with the palm of your hand. Turn the Petal over and repeat the process on the other side until the cut edges are "healed" and appear felted instead of "cut." Rinse out the soap and lay flat to dry. This process should take about 5–7 minutes per Petal. This is a critical step for achieving a finished look.

2. From the silk charmeuse fabric, using pattern pieces E–H, cut:
- Four Back Waistband/Yokes (E) on fold, two for Yoke, two for Yoke Lining
- Four Front Waistband/Yokes (F) on fold, two for Yoke, two for Yoke Lining
- Four Back Bodices (G), two for Back Bodice and two for Back Bodice Lining
- Four Front Bodices (H), two for Front Bodice and two for Front Bodice Lining
- Two Skirt pieces (I), Front and Back, using these measurements:

Size 4: 39" long (lengthwise grain) × 18¾" wide (crosswise grain)
Size 6: 40" long × 18¾" wide
Size 8: 41" long × 19⅛" wide
Size 10: 42" long × 19½" wide
Size 12: 43" long × 19⅞" wide

3. Transfer all pattern markings (E–G) to the wrong side of each of the fabric pieces.

4. From the silk taffeta fabric, cut two Skirt Lining pieces (J) using these measurements:

Size 4: 36" long (lengthwise grain) × 18½" wide (crosswise grain)
Size 6: 37" long × 18½" wide
Size 8: 38" long × 18⅞" wide
Size 10: 39" long × 19⅛" wide
Size 12: 40" long × 19½" wide

5. From the tulle, cut two Underskirt pieces (K) using these measurements:
Size 4: 58" long (lengthwise grain) × 17" wide (crosswise grain)
Size 6: 59" long × 17" wide
Size 8: 60" long × 17⅜" wide
Size 10: 61" long × 17¾" wide
Size 12: 62" long × 18⅛" wide

SEWING INSTRUCTIONS

NOTE: Sew all seams with right sides together, using a ⅝" seam allowance, unless otherwise indicated. Backstitch at the beginning and end of each seam.

1. To prepare the Petals (A–D), mark the center top of each Petal. Measure out 1" on each side of the center. (Figure 1) From the wrong side of the fabric, fold the Petal on the center mark, matching the two 1" marks. Press and stitch the pleat in place for 1⅛" down from the top edge. (For the Row 1 Petals, stitch the pleat for ¾" down from the top edge.) Press the pleat flat with the center mark aligned with the pleat's stitching line; baste the upper edges together ⅛" from the top edge. (Figure 2) Set the Petals aside, keeping the Petals of each size together.

2. Mark the darts and inverted pleats on the Bodice Front and Bodice Front Lining pieces (H). Stitch the darts on the Bodice and Bodice Lining pieces and follow step 1 to fold and stitch the ¾"-wide (and long) inverted pleats at the marks.

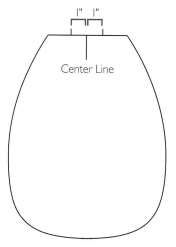

Center Line

Figure 1

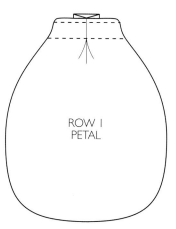

ROW 1 PETAL

Figure 2

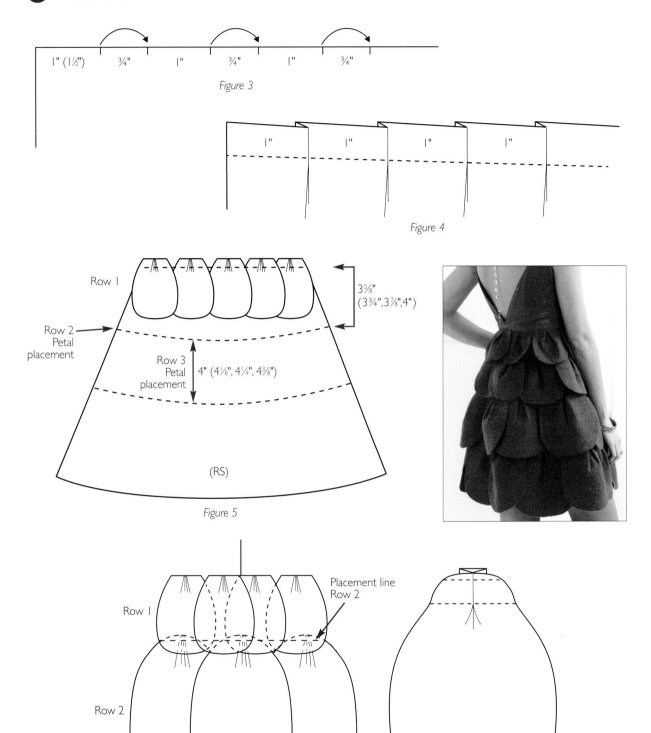

1" (1½")   ¾"   1"   ¾"   1"   ¾"

Figure 3

1"   1"   1"   1"

Figure 4

Row 1

Row 2
Petal
placement

3⅝"
(3¾", 3⅞", 4")

Row 3
Petal
placement

4" (4⅛", 4¼", 4⅜")

(RS)

Figure 5

Row 1

Placement line
Row 2

Row 2

Rows 2–4

Side seam →

Figure 6

3. Sew the Bodice Front pieces **(H)** to the Front Waistband/Yoke **(F)**. Repeat for the Back Bodice **(G)** and Back Waistband/Yoke **(E)**. Sew the Front to the Back at the shoulder seams and right side seam, leaving the left side seam open for the zipper. Repeat for the Front and Back Bodice lining pieces and set aside.

4. On the left side seam of the Skirt Front and Back **(I)**, mark a zipper placement line 6½" below the upper raw edge. Sew the Skirt Front to the Skirt Back, leaving the left side seam open above the zipper placement mark. Press the seams open and finish the seam allowance edges as desired.

5. Mark knife pleats on the top edge of the Skirt Front and Back:
At the top raw edges of the Skirt Front and Skirt Back **(I)**, on the wrong side, mark in 1" from the left raw edge* (sizes 4, 8, and 12), then mark ¾" from that first mark. Mark 1" from the second mark, then mark ¾" from the third mark. Keep alternating your marks: 1", then ¾", 1", then ¾", across the top. The last mark will be 1" from the right raw edge. (Figure 3)
*For sizes 6 and 10, make the first mark 1½" from the left edge, then continue measuring in the 1¾" pattern as above.

6. Match the first 1" mark with the first ¾" mark to form the first pleat as shown in Figure 3. Form the remainder of the pleats (16 pleats each on the Skirt Front and Skirt Back) the same way, matching the 1" mark to the ¾" mark. Pin pleats in place as you fold them. Match the top raw edges of the skirts to the bottom raw edge of the Bodice/Waistbands (Front and Back) and adjust the pleats until the Skirt top edge and the Bodice bottom edge are the same length. (It's best to make very small adjustments, ⅛" or so, to several pleats rather than large adjustments to a couple of pleats.) Press the top edges of the pleats in place and baste across the top of them about ⅜" from the raw edge. (Figure 4) NOTE: Use this same procedure for all dress sizes, adjusting the pleats so the Skirt tops and Bodice bottoms match.

7. Press the pleats down the length of the Skirt so that the pleats get smaller and eventually fade to nothing at approximately 6" from the bottom of the Skirt. To secure the pleats for the Petal placement, you'll baste two placement lines. Baste the Row 2 placement line across the pleats 3⅝" (sizes 4 and 6) from the top edge (size 8: 3¾"; size 10: 3⅞"; size 12: 4"), then stitch the Row 3 placement line 4" (sizes 4 and 6) below the Row 2 line (size 8: 4⅛"; size 10: 4¼"; size 12: 4⅜"). (Figure 5) The pleats will not be as deep on the bottom row of stitching, and there will not be any pleated fabric beneath the bottom (4th) row of Petals.

8. Beginning and ending ⅞" out from the zipper openings on both the Skirt Front and the Skirt Back, arrange the Row 1 Petals on the top edge of the Skirt, overlapping the top Skirt edge ½". Overlap the Petals evenly to arrange five on the Front and five on the Back. (Figure 5) (The Petals will not overlap on the side seams.) Baste the Petals in place.

9. Sew the Front and Back Bodices/Waistbands to the Skirt, matching the right side seam and the left side zipper opening. To hem the Skirt, turn under the bottom raw edge ⅜" and press, then turn under again ⅜" and press. From the wrong side, edgestitch around the hemline close to the top folded edge.

10. Follow the manufacturer's instructions to apply the invisible zipper to the opening on the left side of the dress.

11. Add the Row 2 Petals **(B)** along the Row 2 placement line (Figure 5), under the Row 1 Petals. Starting at the side seam, place the first Petal so the center of the Petal is centered over the side seam. (On the other side, the Petal will be centered over the zipper.) Row 2 Petal placement is staggered so it doesn't match Row 1. Evenly arrange the Row 2 Petals, positioning the top edges of the Petals about 1⅛" above the basting line. (Slightly adjust placement for your size skirt.) Overlap as needed to space the 10 Petals

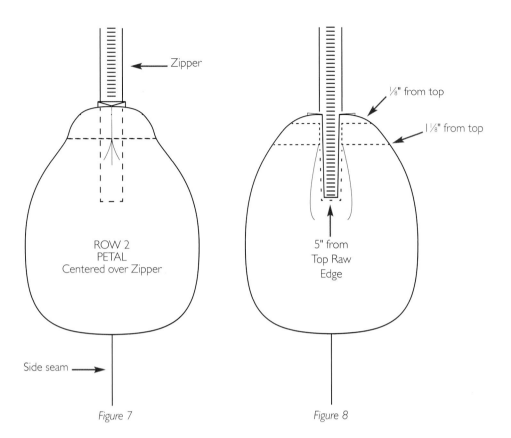

Figure 7

Figure 8

Labels in figures:
- Zipper
- ROW 2 PETAL Centered over Zipper
- Side seam
- ⅛" from top
- 1⅛" from top
- 5" from Top Raw Edge

evenly around the Front and Back of the Skirt, and pin them in place. Sew each Petal in place across the top edge (over the basting stitches) and 1⅛" below the top edge, *except for the Petal over the zipper.* (Figure 6)

12. Baste the Petal that goes over the zipper at the top edge and 1" below the top edge, stopping and starting ¼" to ⅜" from the zipper teeth. (Figure 7) Slice the Petal through the middle of the pleat, down the Petal to ¼" below the bottom of the zipper. Turn under the raw edges of the pleat on each side of the zipper and hand topstitch ⅛" from the folded edge, through all fabric layers. (Figure 8)

13. Follow step 11, excluding the zipper process, to evenly position and stitch the 10 Row 3 Petals **(C)** around the Skirt Front and Back, using the Row 3 placement line as your guide.

14. Mark the Row 4 Petal placement line approximately 4½" below the Row 3 placement line for size 4. (Adjust the distance between the Row 3 and Row 4 placement lines for your dress size according to what is aesthetically pleasing to you.) Repeat step 13 to evenly add the 10 Row 4 Petals **(D)** to the Skirt Front and Back.

15. To assemble the Skirt Lining **(J)**, sew the lining Front and Back pieces together along the side seams, leaving the left seam open above the zipper marking (6½" down from top raw edge). Evenly gather the top edge of the Skirt to fit the waist edge of the Bodice and baste the gathers in place.

16. Sew the Skirt Lining to the Bodice Lining (set aside in step 3) at the waist. Hem the bottom edge of the Skirt Lining with a doubled ½" hem.

17. To add the tulle Underskirt, sew the short edges of the tulle pieces together, leaving the left side seam open above the zipper marking (7½" below the raw edge). Turn the top edge over ½" twice and edgestitch in place (to reinforce the tulle for gathering). Gather the top edge to fit the Skirt Lining. Place the tulle Underskirt over the right side of the Skirt Lining and stitch together at the waist.

18. Sew the lining to the dress along the neckline and armhole edges. Understitch the seam to the lining. Turn to the right side and press all seams flat.

19. Turn the dress inside out and fold the unsewn lining and tulle under along both sides of the zipper and slipstitch in place. ♥

Heart-healthy living

Information, tips, resources, and recipes

Get the facts!

In this book, you've read personal stories from sewing luminaries about their encounters with heart disease and how they look out for their own heart health. Here are some facts that everyone can use to learn more about heart disease and how to fight it.

RED ALERT!

Heart disease is the leading cause of death of women in the United States, but that sobering fact is not common knowledge. Here are a few more eye-opening statistics:

- Both men and women have heart attacks, but they're more often fatal for women.
- Every 90 seconds, a woman in the United States has a heart attack.
- Among all U.S. women who die each year, one in four dies of heart disease.
- In 2004, nearly 60 percent more women died of cardiovascular disease (both heart disease and stroke) than from all cancers combined, and American women are 5 times more likely to die of heart disease than breast cancer.
- More than 10,000 American women younger than 45 have a heart attack every year.

Those are frightening figures, but the good news is that you can take steps to reduce your own risk and educate loved ones.

CHECK IT OUT

One good first step to heart healthiness is to find out how healthy your heart is right now. Here is a list of questions to ask your doctor or nurse when you go for a physical:

What is my risk for heart disease and stroke?

Which screening or diagnostic tests for heart disease do I need, and when?

What can you do to help me quit smoking?

How much physical activity do I need to help protect my heart and blood vessels?

What is a heart-healthy eating plan for me?

What are my numbers and what do they mean?

☐ Blood pressure

☐ Cholesterol
- Total cholesterol
- LDL ("bad") cholesterol
- HDL ("good") cholesterol
- Triglycerides

☐ Body mass index and waist circumference measurement

☐ Blood sugar level

Once you have a baseline for your heart health, you will be able to track changes and improvements. Your doctor should also be able to tell you about various risk factors that may impact your heart health.

♥ DON'T SMOKE

IF YOU DON'T SMOKE, DON'T EVEN THINK ABOUT STARTING.
Smoking carries many health risks beyond heart disease. If you do smoke, make every effort possible to quit. It's the best thing you can do for your health.
Talk to your doctor about resources to help you quit, such as nicotine patches.

KNOW THE SIGNS

Knowing the signs of a heart attack and what to do when you experience them is one of the most important things you can do for your heart health.

For both women and men, the most common symptom of a heart attack is **pain or discomfort in the center of the chest.** The pain or discomfort can be mild or strong. It can last more than a few minutes, or it can go away and come back.

OTHER COMMON SIGNS OF A
HEART ATTACK INCLUDE:
• Pain or discomfort in one or both arms,
back, neck, jaw, or stomach
• Shortness of breath (feeling like you can't get enough air).
The shortness of breath often occurs before or along
with the chest pain or discomfort.
• Nausea (feeling sick to your stomach) or vomiting
• Feeling faint or woozy
• Breaking out in a cold sweat
• Swelling in feet, ankles, and legs

Women are more likely than men to have these other common signs of a heart attack, particularly shortness of breath, nausea, or vomiting, and pain in the back, neck, or jaw.

WOMEN ARE ALSO MORE LIKELY TO HAVE LESS COMMON SIGNS OF A HEART ATTACK, INCLUDING:
Heartburn • Loss of appetite • Fatigue or weakness
Coughing • Heart flutters

The signs of a heart attack often occur suddenly, but they can also develop slowly over hours, days, and even weeks before a heart attack occurs. The more heart attack signs that you have, the more likely it is that you are having a heart attack. Also, if you've already had a heart attack, your symptoms may not be the same for another one.

Even if you're not sure you're having a heart attack, you should still have it checked out.

If you think you, or someone else, may be having a heart attack, wait no more than a few minutes—five at most—before calling 911.

Exercise your heart

One of the best things you can do for your health is to get active!

Regular exercise can help to maintain a healthy body weight, lower blood pressure, and reduce stress—all of which will lower your risk for heart disease. The good news is that you don't have to run a marathon or climb a mountain. Each week aim to get at least:

♥ **2 HOURS AND 30 MINUTES OF MODERATE PHYSICAL ACTIVITY**
During moderate-intensity activities you should notice an increase in your heart rate, but you should still be able to talk comfortably. An example of a moderate-intensity activity is walking on a level surface at a brisk pace (about 3 to 4 miles per hour). Other examples include leisurely bicycling and moderate housework.

OR

♥ **1 HOUR AND 15 MINUTES OF VIGOROUS PHYSICAL ACTIVITY**
If your heart rate increases a lot and you are breathing so hard that it is difficult to carry on a conversation, you are probably doing vigorous-intensity activity. Examples include jogging, bicycling fast or uphill, and singles tennis.

OR

♥ **A COMBINATION OF MODERATE AND VIGOROUS ACTIVITY**

AND

♥ **MUSCLE-STRENGTHENING ACTIVITIES ON TWO OR MORE DAYS**

ADDED BENEFITS
If you need more reasons to start moving, there is strong evidence that regular physical activity can also lower your risk of:

Stroke	Osteoporosis	Colon cancer
Type 2 diabetes	Depression	Breast cancer
High blood pressure	Unhealthy cholesterol levels	Lung cancer

MAKE TIME FOR YOU
Fun activities like yoga, reading, and dancing can reduce stress on you and your heart.

READ ALL ABOUT IT!
Want to learn more? Here are some great resources for finding more information about heart disease and about the steps you can take to make your daily habits more heart healthy.

THE NATIONAL HEART, LUNG, AND BLOOD INSTITUTE AND *THE HEART TRUTH*®
The Heart Truth is a national awareness and prevention campaign about heart disease in women sponsored by the National Heart, Lung, and Blood Institute (NHLBI), part of the National Institutes of Health of the U.S. Department of Health and Human Services. *The Heart Truth* campaign focuses on the following three areas: professional education, patient education, and public awareness.

CONTACT INFORMATION
www.nhlbi.nih.gov/educational/hearttruth
301-592-8573 • TTY: 240-629-3255
NHLBIinfo@nhlbi.nih.gov

U.S. DEPARTMENT OF HEALTH AND HUMAN SERVICES OFFICE ON WOMEN'S HEALTH
The Office on Women's Health (OWH) offers an award-winning comprehensive website that provide reliable, accurate, commercial-free information on the health of women. They cover more than 800 topics, on issues ranging from adolescent health to reproductive health to healthy aging.

CONTACT INFORMATION
200 Independence Avenue, S.W., Washington, DC 20201
www.womenshealth.gov
800-994-9662 • TDD: 888-220-5446

ACT IN TIME TO HEART ATTACK SIGNS CAMPAIGN
The National Heart Attack Alert Program is an initiative of the National Heart, Lung, and Blood Institute to alert people to the signs of heart attack.

CONTACT INFORMATION
www.nhlbi.nih.gov/actintime
301-592-8573

GO TO THE SOURCE
The above information was provided by the U.S. Department of Health and Human Services Office on Women's Health, which publishes helpful fact sheets:

HEART DISEASE FACT SHEET
www.womenshealth.gov/publications/our-publications/fact-sheet/heart-disease.cfm

HEALTH SNAPSHOT: HEART DISEASE
www.womenshealth.gov/publications/our-publications/fact-sheet/health-snapshot/heart-disease-health-snapshot.pdf

QUESTIONS TO ASK YOUR DOCTOR OR NURSE
www.womenshealth.gov/publications/our-publications/heart-health-stroke-questions.pdf

HEART ATTACK FACTS: WHAT IS A HEART ATTACK?
www.womenshealth.gov/heartattack/facts.cfm?q=what-is-a-heart-attack

PHYSICAL ACTIVITY (EXERCISE) FACT SHEET
www.womenshealth.gov/publications/our-publications/fact-sheet/physical-activity.cfm

*Cook red*

You don't have to give up flavor and satisfaction for heart-healthy eating. Swapping a few ingredients can make "delicious" equal cardio friendly.

EAT RIGHT FOR A HEALTHY HEART
Small changes in your diet can make a big difference in your heart health.

BEVERAGES
Take a break from sugary sodas and opt for water with lemon, unsweetened iced tea, or flavored water.

WHOLE GRAINS
Choose whole-grain breads, rice, and noodles, which are packed with important nutrients and are loaded with fiber to make you feel fuller faster.

SODIUM
Excess sodium has been linked to high blood pressure. Cut back on your sodium by limiting restaurant meals, avoiding processed foods, and using spices other than salt. There are plenty of salt-free spice combinations that you can find in your grocery store. It may take a while for you to get used to the taste, but eventually, you should lose your craving for salt.

POTASSIUM
A potassium-rich diet blunts the harmful effects of sodium on blood pressure. Foods rich in potassium include various fruits and vegetables, especially tomatoes and tomato products, orange juice and grapefruit juice, raisins, dates, and prunes, white potatoes and sweet potatoes, bananas, lettuce, and papayas.

APPETIZERS
Instead of being tempted by fried cheese sticks, opt for fresh fruit, sliced veggies, or salad. Salads should contain fresh greens, other fresh vegetables, and chickpeas.

Pass on the high-fat and high-calorie nonvegetable choices, such as bacon, cheese, and croutons. And what better way to top it off than with lemon juice, vinegar, or a reduced-fat or fat-free dressing?

MAIN DISHES
When cooking at home or eating out, look for some key words on menus or in recipes to know you are making healthier choices. Terms like *skinless, broiled, baked, roasted, poached,* or *lightly sautéed* indicate foods that have been prepared in heart-healthy ways.

FRUITS AND VEGETABLES
Try to eat at least five servings of fresh fruits and vegetables each day! Choose a variety of produce to maximize the nutritional benefits and keep your plate interesting.

DESSERTS
Although it's probably okay to order that French silk pie for a special occasion, there are plenty of other yummy alternatives to satisfy your sweet tooth. Try fresh fruit, fat-free frozen yogurt, sherbet, or sorbet. If you must indulge, split your dessert with a friend.

♥ DON'T STRESS
Excess stress can raise your blood pressure and increase your risk of a heart attack. Find healthy ways to cope with stress. Lower your stress level by talking to your friends, exercising, or writing in a journal.

SOUPS

MEXICAN POZOLE
Try this hearty Mexican soup.

INGREDIENTS
2 lb lean beef, cubed*
1 Tbsp olive oil
1 large onion, chopped
1 clove garlic, finely chopped
¼ tsp salt
⅛ tsp pepper
¼ C cilantro
1 can (15 oz) stewed tomatoes
2 oz tomato paste
1 can (1 lb 13 oz) hominy
*Skinless, boneless chicken breasts can be used instead of beef cubes.

DIRECTIONS
1. In large pot, heat oil, then sauté beef.
2. Add onion, garlic, salt, pepper, cilantro, and enough water to cover meat. Cover pot and cook over low heat until meat is tender.
3. Add tomatoes and tomato paste. Continue cooking for about 20 minutes.
4. Add hominy and continue cooking over low heat for another 15 minutes, stirring occasionally. If too thick, add water for desired consistency. ♥

➤ Yield: 10 servings • Serving size: 1 cup

NUTRITION INFORMATION

CALORIES: 253	
TOTAL FAT: 10 GRAMS	
SATURATED FAT: 3 GRAMS	
CHOLESTEROL: 52 MILLIGRAMS	
SODIUM: 425 MILLIGRAMS	
TOTAL FIBER: 4 GRAMS	
PROTEIN: 22 GRAMS	
CARBOHYDRATES: 19 GRAMS	
POTASSIUM: 485 MILLIGRAMS	

MINESTRONE SOUP

A cholesterol-free version of the classic Italian soup, brimming with fiber-rich beans, peas, and carrots

INGREDIENTS

¼ C olive oil

1 clove garlic, minced (or ⅛ tsp powder)

1⅓ C onion, coarsely chopped

1½ C celery with leaves, coarsely chopped

1 can (6 oz) tomato paste

1 Tbsp fresh parsley, chopped

1 C carrots, sliced, fresh or frozen

4¾ C cabbage, shredded

1 can (1 lb) tomatoes, cut up

1 C canned red kidney beans, drained, rinsed

1½ C frozen peas

1½ C fresh green beans dash hot sauce

11 C water

2 C spaghetti, uncooked, broken

DIRECTIONS

1. Heat oil in 4-quart saucepan. Add garlic, onion, and celery, and sauté for about 5 minutes.
2. Add all remaining ingredients except spaghetti. Stir until ingredients are well mixed.
3. Bring to boil and reduce heat, cover, and simmer for about 45 minutes or until vegetables are tender.
4. Add uncooked spaghetti and simmer for only 2–3 minutes. ❤

➤Yield: 16 servings • Serving size: 1 cup

NUTRITION INFORMATION

CALORIES: 112

TOTAL FAT: 4 GRAMS

SATURATED FAT: 0 GRAMS

CHOLESTEROL: 0 MILLIGRAMS

SODIUM: 202 MILLIGRAMS

TOTAL FIBER: 4 GRAMS

PROTEIN: 4 GRAMS

CARBOHYDRATES: 17 GRAMS

POTASSIUM: 393 MILLIGRAMS

CANNERY ROW SOUP

Fish and clam juice give this soup a taste of the sea.

INGREDIENTS

2 lb varied fish fillets (such as haddock, perch, flounder, cod, sole), cut into 1-inch cubes

2 Tbsp olive oil

1 clove garlic, minced

3 carrots, cut in thin strips

2 C celery, sliced

½ C onion, chopped

¼ C green peppers, chopped

1 can (28 oz) whole tomatoes, cut up, with liquid

1 C clam juice

¼ tsp dried thyme, crushed

¼ tsp dried basil, crushed

⅛ tsp black pepper

¼ C fresh parsley, minced

DIRECTIONS

1. Heat oil in large saucepan. Sauté garlic, carrots, celery, onion, and green pepper in oil for 3 minutes.
2. Add remaining ingredients, except parsley and fish. Cover and simmer for 10–15 minutes or until vegetables are fork tender.
3. Add fish and parsley. Simmer covered for 5–10 minutes more or until fish flakes easily and is opaque. Serve hot. ❤

➤Yield: 8 servings • Serving size: 1 cup

NUTRITION INFORMATION

CALORIES: 170

TOTAL FAT: 5 GRAMS

SATURATED FAT: LESS THAN 1 GRAM

CHOLESTEROL: 56 MILLIGRAMS

SODIUM: 380 MILLIGRAMS

TOTAL FIBER: 3 GRAMS

PROTEIN: 22 GRAMS

CARBOHYDRATES: 9 GRAMS

POTASSIUM: 710 MILLIGRAMS

MAIN DISHES

CLASSIC MACARONI AND CHEESE

This recipe proves you don't have to give up your favorite dishes to eat heart-healthy meals. Here's a lower-fat version of a true classic.

INGREDIENTS

2 C macaroni, uncooked

½ C onions, chopped

½ C evaporated skim milk

1 medium egg, beaten

¼ tsp black pepper

1¼ C (4 oz) lowfat sharp cheddar cheese, finely shredded as needed

Nonstick cooking spray

DIRECTIONS

1. Cook macaroni according to directions—but do not add salt to the cooking water. Drain and set aside.
2. Spray casserole dish with nonstick cooking spray.
3. Preheat oven to 350°F.
4. Lightly spray saucepan with nonstick cooking spray. Add onions to saucepan and sauté for about 3 minutes.
5. In another bowl, combine macaroni, onions, and rest of the ingredients, and mix thoroughly.
6. Transfer mixture into casserole dish.
7. Bake for 25 minutes or until bubbly. Let stand for 10 minutes before serving. ❤

➤Yield: 8 Servings • Serving size: ½ cup

NUTRITION INFORMATION

CALORIES: 200

TOTAL FAT: 4 GRAMS

SATURATED FAT: 2 GRAMS

CHOLESTEROL: 34 MILLIGRAMS

SODIUM: 120 MILLIGRAMS

TOTAL FIBER: 1 GRAM

PROTEIN: 11 GRAMS

CARBOHYDRATES: 29 GRAMS

POTASSIUM: 119 MILLIGRAMS

STIR-FRIED BEEF AND CHINESE VEGETABLES

This dish uses very little oil.

INGREDIENTS

2 Tbsp dry red wine
1 Tbsp soy sauce
½ tsp sugar
1½ tsp ginger root, peeled, grated
1 lb boneless round steak, fat trimmed, cut across grain into 1½-inch strips
2 Tbsp vegetable oil
2 medium onions, each cut into 8 wedges
½ lb fresh mushrooms, rinsed, trimmed, sliced
2 stalks (½ C) celery, bias cut into ¼-inch slices
2 small green peppers, cut into thin lengthwise strips
1 C water chestnuts, drained, sliced
2 Tbsp cornstarch
¼ C water

DIRECTIONS

1. Prepare marinade by mixing together wine, soy sauce, sugar, and ginger.
2. Marinate meat in mixture while preparing vegetables.
3. Heat 1 tablespoon oil in large skillet or wok. Stir-fry onions and mushrooms for 3 minutes over medium-high heat.
4. Add celery and cook for 1 minute. Add remaining vegetables and cook for 2 minutes or until green pepper is tender but crisp. Transfer vegetables to warm bowl.
5. Add remaining 1 tablespoon oil to skillet. Stir-fry meat in oil for about 2 minutes, or until meat loses its pink color.
6. Blend cornstarch and water. Stir into meat. Cook and stir until thickened. Then return vegetables to skillet. Stir gently and serve. ❤

➤Yield: 6 servings • Serving size: 6 oz

NUTRITION INFORMATION

|---|---|
CALORIES: 200	
TOTAL FAT: 9 GRAMS	
SATURATED FAT: 2 GRAMS	
CHOLESTEROL: 40 MILLIGRAMS	
SODIUM: 201 MILLIGRAMS	
TOTAL FIBER: 3 GRAMS	
PROTEIN: 17 GRAMS	
CARBOHYDRATES: 12 GRAMS	
POTASSIUM: 552 MILLIGRAMS	

SUMMER VEGETABLE SPAGHETTI

This lively vegetarian pasta is delicious hot or cold!

INGREDIENTS

2 C small yellow onions, cut in eighths
2 C (about 1 lb) ripe tomatoes, peeled, chopped
2 C (about 1 lb) yellow and green squash, thinly sliced
1½ C (about ½ lb) fresh green beans, cut
⅔ C water
2 Tbsp fresh parsley, minced
1 clove garlic, minced
½ tsp chili powder
¼ tsp salt to taste
Black pepper
1 can (6 oz) tomato paste
1 lb spaghetti, uncooked
½ C Parmesan cheese, grated

DIRECTIONS

1. Combine first 10 ingredients in large saucepan. Cook for 10 minutes, then stir in tomato paste. Cover and cook gently for 15 minutes, stirring occasionally, until vegetables are tender.
2. Cook spaghetti in unsalted water according to package directions.
3. Spoon sauce over drained hot spaghetti. Sprinkle Parmesan cheese on top. ❤

➤Yield: 9 servings • Serving size: 1 cup of spaghetti and ¾ cup of sauce with vegetables

NUTRITION INFORMATION

CALORIES: 271
TOTAL FAT: 3 GRAMS
SATURATED FAT: 1 GRAM
CHOLESTEROL: 4 MILLIGRAMS
SODIUM: 328 MILLIGRAMS
TOTAL FIBER: 5 GRAMS
PROTEIN: 11 GRAMS
CARBOHYDRATES: 51 GRAMS
POTASSIUM: 436 MILLIGRAMS

BAKED PORK CHOPS

These are made spicy and moist with egg whites, evaporated milk, and a lively blend of herbs.

INGREDIENTS

6 lean center-cut pork chops, ½-inch thick*
1 egg white
1 C evaporated skim milk
¾ C cornflake crumbs
¼ C fine dry bread crumbs
4 tsp paprika
2 tsp oregano
¾ tsp chili powder
½ tsp garlic powder
½ tsp black pepper
⅛ tsp cayenne pepper
⅛ tsp dry mustard
½ tsp salt as needed
Nonstick cooking spray
*Try the recipe with skinless, boneless chicken or turkey parts, or fish—bake for just 20 minutes.

DIRECTIONS

1. Preheat oven to 375°F.
2. Trim fat from pork chops.
3. Beat egg white with evaporated skim milk. Place chops in milk mixture and let stand for 5 minutes, turning once.
4. Meanwhile, mix cornflake crumbs, bread crumbs, spices, and salt.
5. Use nonstick cooking spray on 13" x 9" baking pan.
6. Remove chops from milk mixture and coat thoroughly with crumb mixture.
7. Place chops in pan and bake at 375°F for 20 minutes. Turn chops and bake for additional 15 minutes or until no pink remains. ❤

➤Yield: 6 servings • Serving size: 1 chop

NUTRITION INFORMATION

CALORIES: 216
TOTAL FAT: 8 GRAMS
SATURATED FAT: 3 GRAMS
CHOLESTEROL: 62 MILLIGRAMS
SODIUM: 346 MILLIGRAMS
TOTAL FIBER: 1 GRAM
PROTEIN: 25 GRAMS
CARBOHYDRATES: 10 GRAMS
POTASSIUM: 414 MILLIGRAMS

CHICKEN & SPANISH RICE

This peppy dish is moderate in sodium, but high in taste!

INGREDIENTS

1 C onions, chopped
¼ C green peppers
2 tsp vegetable oil
1 can (8 oz) tomato sauce*
1 tsp parsley, chopped
½ tsp black pepper
1¼ tsp garlic, minced
5 C cooked rice (in unsalted water)
3½ C chicken breast, cooked, skin and
    bone removed, diced
*Reduce sodium by using one 4-oz can of no-salt-added tomato sauce and one 4-oz can of regular tomato sauce. New sodium content for each serving is 226 mg.

DIRECTIONS

1. In large skillet, sauté onions and green peppers in oil for 5 minutes on medium heat.
2. Add tomato sauce and spices. Heat through.
3. Add cooked rice and chicken, and heat through. ❤

➤Yield: 5 servings • Serving size: 1½ cups

NUTRITION INFORMATION

CALORIES: 406

TOTAL FAT: 6 GRAMS

SATURATED FAT: 2 GRAMS

CHOLESTEROL: 75 MILLIGRAMS

SODIUM: 367 MILLIGRAMS

TOTAL FIBER: 2 GRAMS

PROTEIN: 33 GRAMS

CARBOHYDRATES: 52 GRAMS

POTASSIUM: 527 MILLIGRAMS

SIDE DISHES

GREEN BEANS SAUTÉ

In this dish, green beans and onions are lightly sautéed in just 1 tablespoon of oil.

INGREDIENTS

1 lb fresh or frozen green beans, cut in
    1-inch pieces
1 Tbsp vegetable oil
1 large yellow onion, halved lengthwise,
    thinly sliced
½ tsp salt
½ tsp black pepper
1 Tbsp fresh parsley, minced

DIRECTIONS

1. If using fresh green beans, cook in boiling water for 10–12 minutes or steam for 2–3 minutes until barely fork tender. Drain well. If using frozen green beans, thaw first.
2. Heat oil in large skillet. Sauté onion until golden.
3. Stir in green beans, salt, and pepper. Heat through.
4. Before serving, toss with parsley. ❤

➤Yield: 4 servings • Serving size: ¼ cup

NUTRITION INFORMATION

CALORIES: 64

TOTAL FAT: 4 GRAMS

SATURATED FAT: LESS THAN 1 GRAM

CHOLESTEROL: 0 MILLIGRAMS

SODIUM: 282 MILLIGRAMS

TOTAL FIBER: 3 GRAMS

PROTEIN: 2 GRAMS

CARBOHYDRATES: 8 GRAMS

POTASSIUM: 161 MILLIGRAMS

GOOD-FOR-YOU CORNBREAD

This is good, heart-healthy comfort food!

INGREDIENTS

1 C cornmeal
1 C flour
¼ C white sugar
1 tsp baking powder
1 C 1% fat buttermilk
1 egg, whole
¼ C tub margarine
1 tsp vegetable oil (to grease baking pan)

DIRECTIONS

1. Preheat oven to 350°F.
2. Mix together cornmeal, flour, sugar, and baking powder.
3. In another bowl, combine buttermilk and egg. Beat lightly.
4. Slowly add buttermilk and egg mixture to dry ingredients.
5. Add margarine, and mix by hand or with mixer for 1 minute.
6. Bake for 20–25 minutes in an 8" × 8" greased baking dish. Cool. Cut into 10 squares. ❤

➤Yield: 10 servings • Serving size: 1 square

NUTRITION INFORMATION

CALORIES: 178

TOTAL FAT: 6 GRAMS

SATURATED FAT: 1 GRAM

CHOLESTEROL: 22 MG

SODIUM: 94 MILLIGRAMS

TOTAL FIBER: 1 GRAM

PROTEIN: 4 GRAMS

CARBOHYDRATES: 27 GRAMS

POTASSIUM: 132 MILLIGRAMS

SALAD DRESSING

YOGURT SALAD DRESSING
So easy—so healthy—try it!

INGREDIENTS
8 oz fat-free plain yogurt
¼ C fat-free mayonnaise
2 Tbsp chives, dried
2 Tbsp dill, dried
2 Tbsp lemon juice

DIRECTIONS
1. Mix all ingredients in bowl and refrigerate. ❤

➤ Yield: 8 servings • Serving size: 2 tablespoons

NUTRITION INFORMATION
CALORIES: 23
TOTAL FAT: 0 GRAMS
SATURATED FAT: 0 GRAMS
CHOLESTEROL: 1 MILLIGRAM
TOTAL FIBER: 0 GRAMS
SODIUM: 84 MILLIGRAMS
PROTEIN: 2 GRAMS
CARBOHYDRATES: 4 GRAMS
POTASSIUM: 104 MILLIGRAMS

DESSERTS

APPLE COFFEE CAKE
Apples & raisins keep this cake moist—which means less oil and more health.

INGREDIENTS
5 C tart apples, cored, peeled, chopped
1 C sugar
1 C dark raisins
½ C pecans, chopped
¼ C vegetable oil
2 tsp vanilla
1 egg, beaten
2 C all-purpose flour, sifted
1 tsp baking soda
2 tsp ground cinnamon

DIRECTIONS
1. Preheat oven to 350°F.
2. Lightly oil 13" x 9" x 2" pan.
3. In large mixing bowl, combine apples with sugar, raisins, and pecans. Mix well and let stand for 30 minutes.
4. Stir in oil, vanilla, and egg. Sift together flour, soda, and cinnamon, and stir into apple mixture about a third at a time—just enough to moisten dry ingredients.
5. Turn batter into pan. Bake for 35–40 minutes. Cool cake slightly before serving. ❤

➤ Yield: 20 servings • Serving size: 1 3½-inch by 2½-inch piece

NUTRITION INFORMATION
CALORIES: 196
TOTAL FAT: 8 GRAMS
SATURATED FAT: 1 GRAM
CHOLESTEROL: 11 MILLIGRAMS
SODIUM: 67 MILLIGRAMS
TOTAL FIBER: 2 GRAMS
PROTEIN: 3 GRAMS
CARBOHYDRATES: 31 GRAMS
POTASSIUM: 136 MILLIGRAMS

WINTER CRISP
Only 1 tablespoon of margarine is used to make the crumb topping of this cholesterol-free, tart and tangy dessert. Substitute frozen blueberries and peaches for a summer crisp!

INGREDIENTS
FOR FILLING
½ C sugar
3 Tbsp all-purpose flour
1 tsp lemon peel, grated
¾ tsp lemon juice
5 C apples, unpeeled, sliced
1 C cranberries

FOR TOPPING
⅔ C rolled oats
⅓ C brown sugar, packed
¼ C whole wheat flour
2 tsp ground cinnamon
1 Tbsp soft margarine, melted

DIRECTIONS
1. Prepare filling by combining sugar, flour, and lemon peel in medium bowl. Mix well. Add lemon juice, apples, and cranberries. Stir to mix. Spoon into 6-cup baking dish.
2. Prepare topping by combining oats, brown sugar, flour, and cinnamon in small bowl. Add melted margarine. Stir to mix.
3. Sprinkle topping over filling. Bake in 375°F oven for approximately 40–50 minutes or until filling is bubbly and top is brown. Serve warm or at room temperature. ❤

➤ Yield: 6 servings • Serving size: 1 ¾-inch by 2-inch piece

NUTRITION INFORMATION
CALORIES: 252
TOTAL FAT: 2 GRAMS
SATURATED FAT: LESS THAN 1 GRAM
CHOLESTEROL: 0 MILLIGRAMS
SODIUM: 29 MILLIGRAMS
TOTAL FIBER: 5 GRAMS
PROTEIN: 3 GRAMS
CARBOHYDRATES: 58 GRAMS
POTASSIUM: 221 MILLIGRAMS

OLD-FASHIONED BREAD PUDDING WITH APPLE-RAISIN SAUCE

This old-fashioned treat has been updated with a healthy spin. The sweet but healthy apple-raisin sauce makes a perfect topping.

INGREDIENTS

FOR BREAD PUDDING
10 slices whole wheat bread
3 egg whites
1½ C skim milk
¼ C white sugar
2 tsp white sugar
¼ C brown sugar
1 tsp vanilla extract
½ tsp cinnamon
¼ tsp nutmeg
¼ tsp clove as needed
Vegetable oil spray

FOR APPLE-RAISIN SAUCE
1¼ C apple juice
½ C apple butter
2 Tbsp molasses
½ C raisins
¼ tsp ground cinnamon
¼ tsp ground nutmeg
½ tsp orange zest (optional)

DIRECTIONS

To prepare bread pudding:
1. Preheat oven to 350°F.
2. Spray 8" × 8" baking dish with vegetable oil spray. Lay slices of bread in baking dish in two rows, overlapping like shingles.
3. In medium bowl, beat together egg, egg whites, milk, the ¼ cup of white sugar, brown sugar, and vanilla. Pour egg mixture over bread.
4. In small bowl, stir together cinnamon, nutmeg, clove, and the 2 teaspoons of white sugar.

5. Sprinkle spiced sugar mix over bread pudding. Bake pudding for 30–35 minutes, until it has browned on top and is firm to touch. Serve warm or at room temperature with warm apple-raisin sauce. ❤
➤Yield for bread pudding: 9 servings

To prepare apple-raisin sauce:
1. Stir all ingredients together in medium saucepan.
2. Bring to simmer over low heat. Let simmer for 5 minutes. Serve warm. ❤
➤Yield for apple-raisin sauce: 2 cups
• Serving size: ½ cup

NUTRITION INFORMATION

CALORIES: 233	
TOTAL FAT: 3 GRAMS	
SATURATED FAT: 1 GRAM	
CHOLESTEROL: 24 MILLIGRAMS	
SODIUM: 252 MILLIGRAMS	
TOTAL FIBER: 3 GRAMS	
PROTEIN: 7 GRAMS	
CARBOHYDRATES: 46 GRAMS	
POTASSIUM: 390 MILLIGRAMS	

FRUIT SKEWERS WITH YOGURT DIP

Tangy fruit and sweet yogurt make a perfect taste combination.

INGREDIENTS

1 C strawberries, rinsed, stems removed, and cut in half
1 C fresh pineapple, diced (or canned pineapple chunks in juice, drained)
½ C blackberries
1 tangerine or Clementine, peeled and cut into 8 segments
8 6-inch wooden skewers*
*Skewers have sharp edges, so monitor younger children while eating, or take the fruit off the skewers for them.

FOR DIP
1 C strawberries, rinsed, stems removed, and cut in half
¼ C fat-free plain yogurt
⅛ tsp vanilla extract
1 Tbsp honey

DIRECTIONS

1. Thread two strawberry halves, two pineapple chunks, two blackberries, and one tangerine segment on each skewer.
2. To prepare the dip, puree strawberries in a blender or food processor. Add yogurt, vanilla, and honey, and mix well.
3. Serve two skewers with yogurt dip on the side. Younger children can rinse the fruit, thread onto skewers, and mix the dip. Older children can make the recipe themselves. ❤
➤Yield: 4 servings • Serving size: 2 skewers, 1½ Tbsp dip

NUTRITION INFORMATION

CALORIES: 71	
TOTAL FAT: 0 GRAMS	
SATURATED FAT: 0 GRAMS	
CHOLESTEROL: 0 MILLIGRAMS	
SODIUM: 10 MILLIGRAMS	
TOTAL FIBER: 2 GRAMS	
PROTEIN: 1 GRAM	
CARBOHYDRATES: 18 GRAMS	
POTASSIUM: 174 MILLIGRAMS	

Sewing Basics

Here are the basics you'll need to know to make the projects in this book. The artwork in this section is courtesy of *Vogue® Sewing* from Sixth&Spring Books.

GENERAL SEWING SUPPLIES

Tracing paper

WAX-FREE Tracing Paper
Papel de Calco SIN CERA

Sewing machine needles

Quilting pins

Hand-sewing needles

Thread clips

Measuring tape

Straight pins

Tracing wheel

Fabric shears

Sewing scissors

Iron

Markers and pencils

Seam ripper

METRIC CONVERSIONS
1 inch = 2.540 centimeters
1 yard = .9144 meters
1 centimeter = .3937 inches
1 meter = 3.281 feet/
1.094 yards

FABRIC TERMINOLOGY

Grain refers to the direction the threads in woven fabric run; crosswise threads run under and over the sturdier lengthwise threads.

Lengthwise (straight) grain runs parallel to the selvage. It is the strongest, most stable grain and has the least amount of give in the weave.

Crosswise grain runs from selvage to selvage, weaving under and over the lengthwise grain threads, and has a bit of give.

Bias refers to any diagonal intersection of the lengthwise and crosswise grain threads. **True bias** is obtained by folding the lengthwise edge of the fabric diagonally so the crosswise threads are parallel to the selvage edge.

Selvage is the flat woven border with a prefinished edge that runs along the edges of the lengthwise grain.

FABRIC PREPARATION
• Before beginning any project, you must first prepare the fabric.
• Wash, dry, and steam press your fabric to remove any wrinkles and fold lines. Washing and drying will also pre-shrink any fabric that needs it, and steam pressing will straighten the lengthwise and crosswise grains as needed.

TIPS FOR CUTTING FABRIC
• Prepare the fabric before cutting it.
• When cutting fabric with scissors, use long, bent-handled shears and keep the bottom blade in contact with the cutting surface while cutting.
• Cut each fabric piece the number of times specified in the instructions or on the pattern.
• Transfer all markings (such as for pleats, stitching lines, fold lines, etc.) using the marking tool(s) of your choice.

PRESSING TIPS
• First press the stitching line flat to blend the stitches into the fabric, then press the seam open (if directed).
• For enclosed seams (in cuffs and flaps), first press the seam open from the wrong side then turn and press flat from the right side.

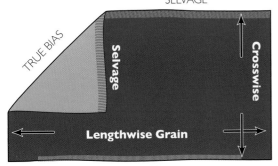

SELVAGE

TRUE BIAS

Selvage

Crosswise

Lengthwise Grain

SELVAGE

Figure 1

BASIC STITCHES

Backstitching is done at the beginning and end of a seam. Take a couple of stitches forward, then reverse for a couple of stitches, then continue to stitch forward.

Basting stitches are long stitches that can be made by hand or machine and are used to temporarily secure layers of fabric together so they remain stable while seams are sewn.

A **slipstitch** is a nearly invisible hand-sewing stitch used to hem and attach linings. Slide the needle through the folded edge and at the same point, pick up a thread of the under fabric. Continue stitching in this manner, taking stitches $1/8$" to $1/4$" apart, spacing the stitches evenly.

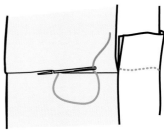

Figure 2

Staystitching is used in areas that might otherwise stretch during the construction process. You'll use a slightly longer stitch than the one you'll use for your seams and will stitch $1/8$" inside the seamline.

A **straight stitch** is the most basic stitch and the one you'll use for virtually all seams.

Topstitching (right) is decorative stitch that both emphasizes structural details and keeps seams and edges flat and crisp.

Edgestitching is topstitching placed very close to a finished edge.

See page 79

Understitching prevents facings from rolling to the outside of your finished piece. Press the seam allowance toward the facing. From the right side of the facing, stitch through the facing and seam allowance $1/8$" away from the seam line.

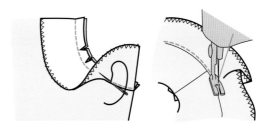

Figure 3

Zigzag stitching looks exactly like its name and is used to finish the raw edges of cut pieces to prevent them from unraveling.

MAKING A BIAS BINDING STRIP

Bias binding is used to finish the edges of several apparel and fashion accessory projects.

1. Take a rectangular piece of fabric cut on the straight (lengthwise) grain and fold the fabric diagonally at one end to find the true bias. (Figure 1)

2. Using the bias fold as your guide, mark parallel lines on the fabric that are the width of your bias binding strip. Mark as many bias strips as needed to make your desired length binding strip, allowing for a ¼" seam allowance. (Figure 4)

3. Cut away the triangular ends but do not cut along the marked lines. (Figure 4)

4. On the marked fabric (step 2 above), join the shorter ends with right sides together; one strip will extend beyond the edge at each side. (Figure 5)

5. Stitch a ¼" seam and press it open.

6. Begin cutting on the marked line at one end and continue cutting in a circular fashion. (Figure 6)

PREPARING THE BIAS BINDING STRIP

1. Cut and stitch your binding strips per the instructions for your project; then press the seams flat.

2. With wrong sides together, fold the strip in half lengthwise and press lightly. Open the strip, lay it wrong side up, and fold each raw edge in toward the pressed center fold; press. (Figure 7)

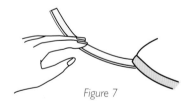

Figure 7

See page 113

APPLYING THE BIAS BINDING STRIP

If you are applying the binding around corners you will have to miter the corners to keep them from being too bulky; see mitering directions below.

1. Lay your binding strip around all the edges it will cover. Adjust its placement to avoid placing the binding's seams at the corners where they'll add too much bulk. Leave at least 1" of the binding strip free at the beginning and end of the application for finishing.

2. Open the binding strip and with right sides together and all raw edges aligned, pin it to the right side of the edge being bound, beginning in the middle of one long edge. (Figure 8) NOTE: If the binding will go around corners, see "Mitering Binding Corners" (opposite) before moving to the next step.

3. Baste the strip with a seam allowance $\frac{1}{8}$" less than the width of the finished binding, then stitch the seam next to, but not on, the basting. Pull the basting threads to remove them.

4. Turn the bias strip over the seam allowance. Pin in place and slipstitch the folded edge of the strip to the item. (Figure 9)

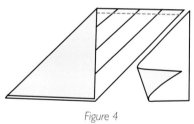

Figure 4

Figure 5

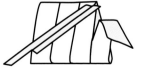

Figure 6

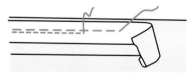

Figure 8

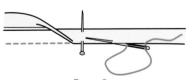

Figure 9

MITERING BINDING CORNERS

Bindings can bunch up in corners, so if you're binding a quilt (or anything with corners), you'll need to miter the strip at the corners to get rid of excess fabric.

1. Open out one pre-folded edge of the binding strip and pin it in place.

2. Stitch to the corner and backstitch for reinforcement. (Figure 10)

3. Fold the strip diagonally, as shown, to bring it around the corner. Pin, then stitch the adjoining edge through the corner from one end to the other end. (Figure 11)

4. Fold the binding to form a miter on the right side and turn the bias strip over the seam allowance. (Figure 12)

5. To finish the mitered corner on the wrong side, form a miter (with the fold of the miter in the opposite direction from the one formed on the right side to evenly distribute the bulk of the miter).

6. Turn, pin, and slipstitch the binding over the seam line, fastening the miter at the corner. (Figure 13)

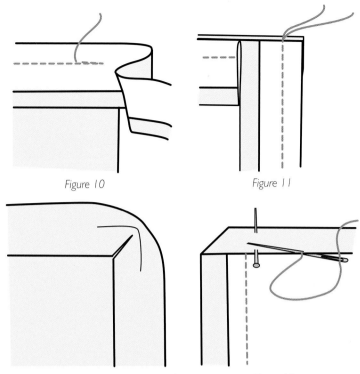

Figure 10

Figure 11

Figure 12

Figure 13

♥ CLEAN FINISHING BINDING STRIPS

Apply the binding up to the edge where it will be clean finished, leaving about 1" of extra binding strip. Trim the excess binding to between ¼" and ⅜" and then fold the raw ends of the binding under, inside the strip. Press.

See page 20

QUILT BINDING

Use this binding method on all wall hangings, table runners, and quilts.

1. Fold the joined strip in half lengthwise with wrong sides together; press.

2. With the quilt top facing up and with raw edges aligned, pin the strip around the perimeter of the quilt. Baste in place ⅜" from the raw edges. (Figure 14)

3. Stitch the binding strip to the quilt using a ½" seam allowance, mitering the corners. (Figure 14) To miter the corners, follow steps 2 to 5 of Mitering Binding Corners.

4. Turn the strip over the seam allowance to the quilt backing and slipstitch in place. (Figure 15)

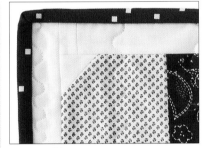

Figure 14

Figure 15

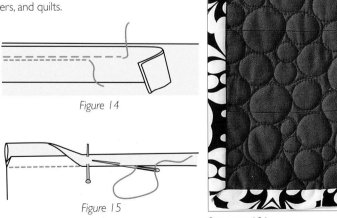

See page 106

Piece of My Heart Pincushion

This adorable pincushion designed by Michèle Filon can be made from scraps of your favorite fabrics. Use it as a reminder to take care of your heart.

FINISHED DIMENSIONS
4½" tall x 5" wide

FABRIC
• Four 6" squares of quilting cotton or fabric of your choice; squares can coordinate, contrast, or match, as your heart desires.

SUPPLIES
• General Sewing Supplies (page 138)
• Matching all-purpose thread
• Fiberfill stuffing
• Tracing paper and pencil
• Ruler

CUTTING THE FABRIC
Use the Heart Template on this page.

1. Pin any two squares together along one edge, with right sides together and raw edges aligned. Stitch a ¼" seam; press the seam open.

2. Lay the two pieced squares flat and, with right sides together and raw edges aligned, position a third square over them so the center of the third square is aligned with the seam joining the two pieced squares. Pin and stitch the seam; press the seam open.

3. Trace the heart template and cut it out. Place the heart template over the seamed squares as desired and trace the outline of the heart directly onto the fabric. Cut the fabric on the traced lines for the front of the pincushion.

4. From the remaining square, use the template to cut out the heart for the back of the pincushion.

SEWING INSTRUCTIONS
1. With right sides together, pin the front to the back with raw edges aligned. Stitch a ¼" seam around the heart, leaving a 2" opening along one straight side for turning and stuffing. Clip all the curves; turn the heart right side out.

2. Stuff the pincushion through the opening until you achieve your desired firmness; hand-stitch the opening closed. ❤

CREDITS

PORTRAITS OF DESIGNERS

p. 12 Allison Michael Orenstein
p. 16 Glasgow Photography
  (Beaver Dam, WI)
p. 20 Moda
p. 23 Melinda Smith
p. 26 Jon Zabala for
  French General
p. 29 Jack Deutsch
p. 32 Ross Kennedy
p. 37 Allison Tyler Jones
p. 42 Kimberly Saba
p. 46 Jerry Mucklow
p. 51 David Butler
p. 54 Debbie Patterson
p. 58 Rose Callahan
p. 61 Contrino Photography
p. 65 Joel T. Rose
p. 68 Cameron McLean
p. 79 Christin Polomsky
p. 86 Sweetwater
p. 90 David Butler
p. 96 Jimmy Abegg
p. 99 Robin Harmening
p. 109 Sophia Young
p. 113 Arcata Photo
p. 119 Stuart Mullenberg

SPECIAL CONTRIBUTORS

Hop! Skip! Jump! (p. 12):
Instructions and diagrams by
Shea Henderson
Parson Gray Ditty Bag (p. 51):
Instructions by Sandy Hussey
Westminster Backpack (p. 74)
and *Petal Dress* (p. 119):
Instructions by Carol R. Zentgraf
Petal Dress (p. 119):
Pattern by Steffani Lincecum

FASHION RESOURCES

Josie Maran Cosmetics

From *Knit Red* by Laura Zander
• *Village Bag* (p. 37):
Ruffled Pullover
by Kim Hargreaves
• *Fleur Rouge Quilt* (p. 46):
L-Shaped Stole
by Barbara Venishnick
• *Sweet Sixteen Skirt*
(pp. 79, 81–82):
Lace Hearts Cardi
by Martin Storey

ABOUT THE AUTHOR

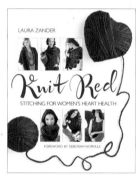

LAURA ZANDER

is the co-founder and co-owner of Jimmy Beans Wool (jimmybeanswool.com), which was named by *Inc.* magazine as one of the 5,000 fastest growing private companies in the United States for four years (2009, 2010, 2011, and 2012), and is the first official yarn supplier to the U.S. Olympic Snowboarding and Freeskiing teams for the 2014 Olympics. Zander was named one of ten national winners of Ernst & Young Entrepreneurial Winning Women for 2011. She is also the author of *Knit Red* (Sixth&Spring Books, 2012), which she conceived and wrote as part of her Stitch Red initiative to support The Heart Truth® Foundation to raise awareness and funds to fight heart disease, the number-one killer of women in the United States. Laura lives with her husband, Doug, their son, Huck, and their canine friends in Reno, Nevada. ❤

jimmy beans wool

Sticking it to heart disease.